# Xuan Kong
# Flying
# Stars
## Feng Shui

玄空飛星風水

玄
空
飛
星
風
水

# Xuan Kong Flying Stars Feng Shui

The author can be reached at:

**Mastery Academy of Chinese Metaphysics Sdn. Bhd.** (611143-A)
19-3, The Boulevard, Mid Valley City,
59200 Kuala Lumpur, Malaysia.
Tel      : +603-2284 8080
Fax     : +603-2284 1218
Email  : info@masteryacademy.com
Website: www.masteryacademy.com

DISCLAIMER:

Published by JY Books Sdn. Bhd. (659134-T)

玄空飛星風水

# INDEX

玄
空
飛
星
風
水

## PREFACE

"Disclose not the Secrets of Heaven" 天機不可洩露 (Tian Ji Bu Ke Xie Lou). These 6 words have had an undue influence on the development of Classical Feng Shui for many decades. Despite the advancement that has been made in opening up Classical Feng Shui to the masses through books, classes and Feng Shui schools, you will find that "Disclose not the Secrets of Heaven" lingers behind the scenes. Many books written by Hong Kong and Taiwan masters are notorious for deliberately incorporating misleading information, or for withholding important information from all but 'indoor' students.

"Disclose not the Secrets of Heaven" has never been my approach to Feng Shui. I believe that anyone who is interested in Classical Feng Shui, Xuan Kong or Flying Stars should have the opportunity to learn and understand Flying Stars, and learn it properly, without having to doubt or question the accuracy, validity and truth of the academic information they are receiving. And that has been the driving force behind my decision to write a series of books on Xuan Kong Flying Stars. I believe that the Secrets of Heaven should be available to anyone who wants to know!

I have written this first book in the Xuan Kong Flying Stars series, as both an introductory text for those interested in studying Classical Feng Shui on their own and also for those who would like to do some background reading and grasp the basic fundamentals before attending a proper Classical Feng Shui course, such as the Feng Shui Mastery Module 1.

This book also provides an introduction to Classical Feng Shui for those who are familiar with the 'pop Feng Shui' variant of Flying Stars, which combines Flying Stars with the use of object-based cures. This book will show you how Flying Stars is really used, and how it is possible to make use of Flying Stars WITHOUT any product based cures, or the placement of 'good luck' objects in your home.

If you have read any of my *Feng Shui for Homebuyers* books, in particular, my forthcoming book, ***Feng Shui for Apartment Buyers - Home Owners***, you will find this book affords greater understanding and insight into some of the guidance provided in those books with regards to the use of Flying Stars, particularly in apartments and condominiums.

There are many books that have been written on the subject of Flying Stars. What is different or unique about the Xuan Kong Flying Stars series?

玄空飛星風水

Firstly, this book is written with the benefit of my many years as a Master Trainer at the Mastery Academy of Chinese Metaphysics, teaching students all around the world about Feng Shui and other Chinese Metaphysical subjects like Yi Jing, Qi Men, BaZi and Mian Xiang. In the course of all my years teaching, I have developed a structured, systematic method of teaching Flying Stars. More importantly, I have structured my courses in such a manner that students can start doing something to improve their own Feng Shui, from the end of Day 1 of their first course.

So, by the end of this book, you will have enough Flying Stars knowledge to audit your own house and make small modifications or changes to your property to tap into the timely and positive Qi of Period 8. You will also be reasonably well-versed in the basics of Classical Feng Shui to approach other systems like Eight Mansions Feng Shui (Ba Zhai Feng Shui) or to advance further to a higher level of Flying Stars study, if you so wish.

Secondly, this book not only is written from the standpoint of an educator, but also from the standpoint of a professional consultant. Anyone can learn the theory of Flying Stars, but being able to wield Flying Stars well comes with experience of application. And this is something you will find the Xuan Kong Flying Stars series offers you – academic grounding, coupled with practical understanding. You will not only know the WHYS, but you will also know the 'HOW TO FIX".

I hope you will have as much fun reading this book, and learning Flying Stars, as I had writing this book.

**Joey Yap**
Sydney, July 2007

Author's personal website: www.joeyyap.com
Academy websites: www.masteryacademy.com | www.masteryjournal.com |
www.maelearning.com

玄
空
飛
星
風
水

# MASTERY ACADEMY
## OF CHINESE METAPHYSICS™

At **www.masteryacademy.com**, you will find some useful tools to ascertain key information about the Feng Shui of a property or for the study of Astrology.

To learn more about your personal Destiny, you can use the Joey Yap BaZi Ming Pan Calculator to plot your Four Pillars of Destiny – you just need to have your date of birth (day, month, year) and time of birth. The Joey Yap Flying Stars Calculator can be utilised to plot your home or office Flying Stars chart. To find out your personal best directions, use the 8 Mansions Calculator.

For more information about BaZi, Xuan Kong or Flying Star Feng Shui, or if you wish to learn more about these subjects with Joey Yap, logon to the Mastery Academy of Chinese Metaphysics website at **www.masteryacademy.com.**

**MASTERY ACADEMY**
**E-LEARNING CENTER**
**www.maelearning.com**

**Further your Xuan Kong Flying Stars mastery...with the Mastery Academy's E-Learning Center!**

**www.maelearning.com**

Bookmark this address on your computer, and visit this newly-launched website today. With the E-Learning Center, knowledge of Chinese Metaphysics is a mere `click' away!

Our E-Learning Center consists of 3 distinct components.

### 1. Online Courses
These shall comprise of 3 Programs: our Online Feng Shui Program, Online BaZi Program, and Online Mian Xiang Program. And Flying Stars (Xuan Kong Fei Xing) is one of the topics covered in our Feng Shui Program.

### 2. MA Live!
With MA Live!, Joey Yap's workshops, tutorials, courses and seminars on various Chinese Metaphysics subjects – including Flying Stars - are broadcasted right to your computer screen. Better still, participants will not only get to see and hear Joey talk `live', but also get to engage themselves directly in the event and more importantly, TALK to Joey via the MA Live! interface. All the benefits of a live class, minus the hassle of actually having to attend one!

### 3. Video-On-Demand (VOD)
Get immediate streaming-downloads of the Mastery Academy's wide range of educational DVDs (of which we have a Xuan Kong Flying Stars Series), right on your computer screen. No more shipping costs and waiting time to be incurred!

Study at your own pace, and interact with your Instructor and fellow students worldwide... at your own convenience and privacy. With our E-Learning Center, knowledge of Chinese Metaphysics is brought DIRECTLY to you in all its clarity, with illustrated presentations and comprehensive notes expediting your learning curve!

**Welcome to the Mastery Academy's E-LEARNING CENTER...YOUR virtual gateway to Chinese Metaphysics mastery!**

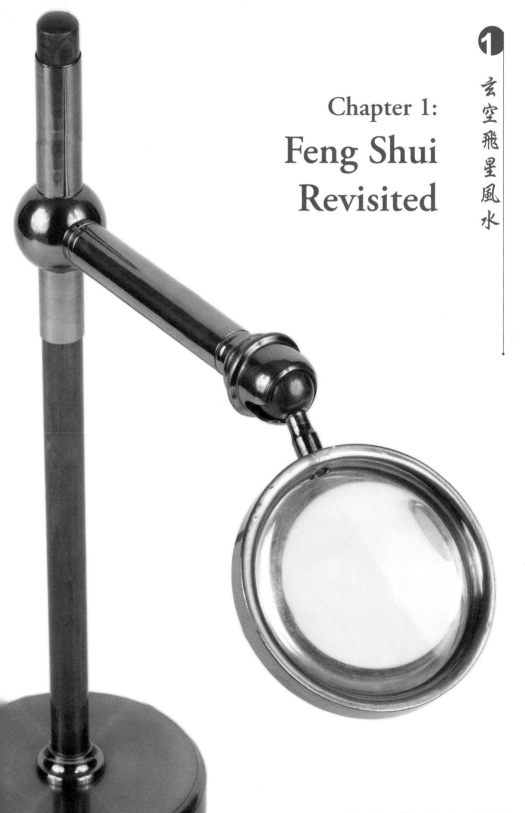

# Chapter 1:
# Feng Shui
# Revisited

玄空飛星風水

The question 'What is Feng Shui' looks on the surface to be a no-brainer question. Surely everyone knows what Feng Shui is? Why is there a need to answer this question?

Honestly, in this day and age, the question 'What is Feng Shui' is unlikely to solicit any kind of consistent answer. Everyone has their own interpretation or answer to the question 'What is Feng Shui'. That is not to say that all those answers are necessarily correct. But at the same time, a definitive answer is not easy in this day and age. Why? Because Feng Shui is no longer the same art it was 2000 years ago, when it was known as Kan Yu (堪輿) and was mostly utilised to select burial grounds.

Feng Shui has evolved. Today, if you visit the Feng Shui section of a bookstore (sometimes labeled as 'alternative' or 'Far East Philosophy'), you'll find books on everything from crystal therapy to interior design to space clearing. So you see, the question 'What is Feng Shui' is in fact quite hard to answer.

I prefer to phrase the question in this manner: What is Classical Feng Shui? Classical Feng Shui first and foremost is my term for Feng Shui that is based on and utilises techniques and methods from classical texts on Feng Shui, such as the Green Satchel Classics 青囊經 (Qing Nang Jing), Earth Discern Study Truth 地理辨正 (Di Li Bian Zhen), Purple White Scripts 紫白訣 (Zi Bai Jue), Earth Entering Eye 入地眼 (Ru Di Yan), and Snow Heart Classics 雪心賦 (Xue Xin Fu) to name a few. Classical Feng Shui is the term I use to encompass both San He (三合) and San Yuan (三元) Feng Shui, the two original schools of Feng Shui.

Classical Feng Shui is about tapping into the natural energies of the environment or Qi in order to improve your life and achieve your goals. This is achieved through the correct placement of doors and the appropriate location of important areas of your home like the kitchen, bedroom and study, within your house based on the natural external environmental features.

Classical Feng Shui is not about objects or decorative items such as crystals, resin dragons or toads. It is not about Ba Gua mirrors above your main door, Mandarin Ducks on your desk and Fu Dogs at your main gate. Classical Feng Shui is not about space clearing or crystal therapy or wearing certain colours to 'enhance your luck'. Classical Feng Shui is not concerned about landscaping your house with certain type of plants, the interior decor of your kitchen, what you put in your handbag or what number your car plate or house number is. And there's no need to steal soil from your rich neighbour's garden to make a 'wealth vase'. Classical Feng Shui makes absolutely no mention of any of these practices.

These practices are more in line with what I call 'New-Age Feng Shui' or 'Pop Feng Shui'. New-Age Feng Shui is more about the psychological effect of objects and symbolism than anything else. New-Age Feng Shui has no consistent principles and its practice is not rooted in any classical theories or texts. Frequently, New-Age Feng Shui is a commercialised derivative or watered down version of certain aspects of Feng Shui sub-systems or misunderstood sound bites of aspects of the Yi Jing or Chinese culture.

玄
空
飛
星
風
水

The Eight Life Aspiration 'system' is a good example of 'New-Age Feng Shui'. This 'system' (which involves some very loose borrowings from the Ba Gua) associates each corner of the house with an aspiration of life. For example – the North is the Career corner, the Southwest is the Love corner, South the Fame corner and so forth. This 'system' requires the use of oriental-styled products and Chinese folklore objects to 'enhance' each aspiration in a house.

The 'Eight Life Aspirations' is not a proper Classical Feng Shui system documented in any of the historical classical texts and literatures. It is, like much of New-Age Feng Shui, a modern and purely commercial invention.

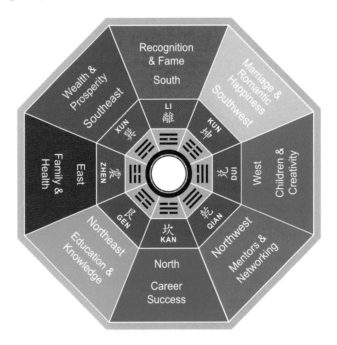

*In the Eight Life Aspiration System, every corner of the home represents an aspiration of your life. This is not a Classical Feng Shui system a pure New-Age or Pop Feng Shui concept.*

玄
空
飛
星
風
水

# Making an Identification

If you are uncertain as to whether or not something is Classical Feng Shui or some form, version, itineration or spin-off of New-Age Feng Shui, there is an easy way to separate them.

Typically, all forms of Classical Feng Shui will have the following characteristics:

a) utilises a Luo Pan (a Feng Shui compass) for the purposes of acquiring specific directions

b) involves the analysis of location and direction (North, South, East, West, Northwest, Northeast, Southwest, Southeast)

c) requires the observation and analysis of Luan Tou or environmental forms and formations, which include but are not limited to mountain shapes, mountain ranges, embrace of land by mountains, flow of water and direction of water

d) takes into account time aspects

e) considers the residents of the property

f) does NOT require the placement of symbolic items, culturally significant figures or good luck objects

g) does NOT involve any spiritual practice or spirituality or any religious or spiritual activities such as chanting, placement of joss sticks or prayers to deities or figurines

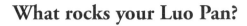

玄
空
飛
星
風
水

# What rocks your Luo Pan?

If you like the psychological aspects of pop Feng
Shui, or if you find it uplifting or motivational,
that is fine. There's a place in this world for all
kinds of people, and by necessity, all kinds of Feng Shui.

But that's not the kind of Feng Shui I practice professionally
and it's not the kind of Feng Shui I teach at the Mastery
Academy of Chinese Metaphysics. So this book may not be for
you if Pop Feng Shui is what interests you and works for you.

But if you are interested in learning a simple easy method in
which to apply Classical Feng Shui, at home or at your office,
then this is the book for you. If you are interested in exploring
what Classical Feng Shui is all about, and in particular, if you
are interested in understanding how you can make use of one
of the sub-systems of Classical Feng Shui, called Xuan Kong
Fei Xing (玄空飛星) or Xuan Kong Flying Stars as it is known
in English, then this is also the book for you.

If you are interested in studying Classical Feng Shui, this is
also the book for you as Xuan Kong Flying Stars is one of the
easiest and most basic systems of Feng Shui to learn. This book
is also an ideal stepping stone into the world of Classical Feng
Shui and beginning your journey into the fascinating field of
Chinese Metaphysics.

玄
空
飛
星
風
水

# The Two Schools

Before we can delve into Xuan Kong Flying Stars, we must first have some background; in particular, an understanding of a certain long-standing (and probably totally unnecessary) 'rivalry' the exists in the world of Classical Feng Shui.

Feng Shui can loosely be classified into two systems or approaches: the Li Qi 理氣 system, also known as Theory and Calculation of Qi system, and the Luan Tou 巒頭 system, also known as Landform Feng Shui System. The Li Qi system is a more calculation-driven approach, and places more emphasis on computing the movement of Qi in a property, and the

quality of Qi at a particular point in time. The Luan Tou system is more focused on the use of Forms such as mountains, rivers and places a great deal of emphasis on finding the Meridian Spot 龍穴 (Long Xue).

You may have heard of this rivalry – it is often incorrectly described in many 'New-Age Feng Shui' books as a division between the 'compass school' and 'forms school'. In fact, there is no such thing as a 'compass school' in Classical Feng Shui. All systems of Classical Feng Shui involve the use of a compass or Luo Pan as it is called in Feng Shui terminology.

Both the Li Qi and Luan Tou systems have methods and techniques to determine the quality of Qi, based on time computations AND require the observation of Forms. Therefore, the division of Feng Shui systems into 'Forms' and 'Compass' divisions is plain wrong.

玄
空
飛
星
風
水

There is of course a difference between the two systems.

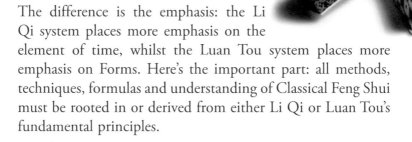

The difference is the emphasis: the Li Qi system places more emphasis on the element of time, whilst the Luan Tou system places more emphasis on Forms. Here's the important part: all methods, techniques, formulas and understanding of Classical Feng Shui must be rooted in or derived from either Li Qi or Luan Tou's fundamental principles.

There are TWO 'schools' (I use the word 'schools' here in the context of schools of thought rather than academic institutions) of Feng Shui that incorporate both Li Qi and Luan Tou: San Yuan 三元 (Three Cycles) and San He 三合 (Three Harmony). But while both San Yuan and San He incorporate principles on Li Qi and Luan Tou, each school has a different emphasis. San Yuan places more emphasis on Li Qi while San He focuses more on Luan Tou.

If a system or technique or method of Feng Shui cannot explain which aspect of San Yuan or San He's fundamental principles it is based on or derived from, then it is probably NOT Classical Feng Shui.

Why do you need to know about this rivalry? Consider it part history lesson, part background knowledge, and part preparation for your advancement to more sophisticated levels of knowledge and practice of Feng Shui.

In all fields of study, contradictions exist. It is important to understand from the onset that there are two systems, and that they do not always agree with each other. It is critical to appreciate that each system has its flaws and strengths.

玄
空
飛
星
風
水

Understanding the flaws and strengths of each system is the key to being able to wield both with ease, and yet know when is the right situation to apply which system.

And of course, there is the practical reason. By appreciating that the rivalry exists (but is somewhat pointless), you will be less at risk of being misled into paying a lot of money to learn 'secret formulas' or 'our school's secrets' because you go into the world of Chinese Metaphysics well aware that there are other methods and techniques, and a whole other major system out there.

You will be aware that all teachers, practitioners and consultants have their preferred methods. But most importantly, by understanding that this rivalry exists (and is exactly that – just a rivalry), you will begin your journey into Feng Shui with the knowledge that there is no 'one system to rule them all'!

玄
空
飛
星
風
水

# Mysterious and Void Flying Stars

Xuan Kong Flying Stars (or Xuan Kong Fei Xing as it is known in Mandarin) is a Feng Shui mini-system that falls under the broader category of Xuan Kong Feng Shui. Xuan Kong Feng Shui itself is a system under the San Yuan school.

Xuan Kong means 'mysterious and void' but don't let that name mislead you – it's really quite a simple and easy to use system and there is nothing 'mysterious' about it.

It does of course, like many fields of Chinese Metaphysics, have levels of sophistication and application. This book will show you the most basic and simple level of application for Xuan Kong Flying Stars. It will also introduce you to the key fundamental principles you will need to learn and understand, in order to not just appreciate Xuan Kong Flying Stars at its highest level but master Xuan Kong, indeed, San Yuan Feng Shui.

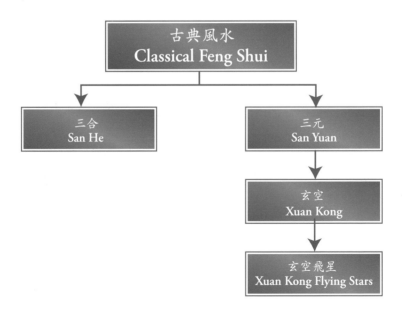

玄
空
飛
星
風
水

# The Flying Stars Origins Story

Another history lesson? Not quite. The Flying Stars Origins story is important because it helps us get the right perspective on Flying Stars Feng Shui. For starters, it's not quite as 'old' as most people think. In fact, Xuan Kong Flying Stars is a relatively 'new' sub-system of Classical Feng Shui. It was mainly developed at the turn of the 20th century.

The problem with Feng Shui is that people assume everything that is associated with Feng Shui has to be (take your pick) either an ancient art, a classical practice or something that has stood the test of time. While that is true with regards to the theories of Classical Feng Shui, the practice is very different and many approaches have been developed (based on the classical theories) to cater to the way we live today.

玄
空
飛
星
風
水

Here's another reason why it's important that you know the 'Origins Story'. You will find there are some people who seek to use historical association or academic association (sometimes called lineage) to support their skills as Feng Shui practitioners or teachers. Without understanding the origins of a Classical Feng Shui systems, it is not possible often to verify these historical or academic associations, and in turn, be certain of the level of skill or knowledge the person has.

Xuan Kong Flying Stars also is a rather unique system because its historical origins are actually documented and can clearly be traced.

No one knows who originated Feng Shui. All we know is that it originated as Kan Yu, a method of selecting burial sites, and has some philosophical and metaphysical aspects. We also know that over the course of the last 2000 years, particularly during the Ming and Qing Dynasties, certain masters like Jiang Da Hong and Zhang Zhong Shan, wrote treatises and books, which have today become regarded as cornerstone texts on specific aspects of Feng Shui and Chinese Metaphysics.

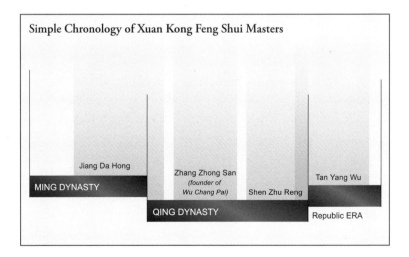

Simple Chronology of Xuan Kong Feng Shui Masters

Jiang Da Hong

MING DYNASTY

Zhang Zhong San
*(founder of Wu Chang Pai)*

Shen Zhu Reng

Tan Yang Wu

QING DYNASTY

Republic ERA

玄空飛星風水

Jiang Da Hong 蔣大鴻 (1616-1714) was a scholar during the late Ming-early Qing Dynasty era. Jiang is famous for having written many important Classical Feng Shui treatises and texts such as Earth Discern Truth Study 地理辨正 (Di Li Bian Zheng), Profound Returning Records 歸厚錄 (Gui Hou Lu), Heavenly Yuan Five Songs 天元五歌 (Tian Yuan Wu Ge), Heavenly Yuan Principles 天元余義 (Tian Yuan Yu Yi), Old Mirror Song 古鏡歌 (Gu Jing Ge) and Water Dragon Classics 水龍經 (Shui Long Jing). At that time, it was unheard of for scholars to disclose their knowledge in this manner. Most scholars of Chinese Metaphysics held onto the mantra that the secrets of heaven should not be disclosed or 天機不可洩露 (Tian Ji Bu Ke Xie Lou).

While Jiang wrote many treatises and texts on the subject of Xuan Kong, he too held to the viewpoint that the secrets of heaven should not be disclosed. So he wrote his treatises and texts on Xuan Kong in flowery, poetic but mostly cryptic language that made it virtually impossible to figure out what he was saying.

It was only until a late Qing Dynasty Imperial Scholar, Zhang Zhong Shan 章仲山, added commentaries to Jiang's works, that the information and knowledge about Xuan Kong became more accessible. Zhang then founded his own school, Wu Chang Pai 無常派, that focused on Xuan Kong Feng Shui. From Wu Chang Pai came many famous masters. One of them was Tan Yang Wu 談養吾, who could be said to be one of the first scholar-practitioners of Xuan Kong Flying Stars.

玄空飛星風水

Being a student of the school, Tan had the benefit of observing the practice of Xuan Kong and also, any oral instructions that his teacher may have shared with him, which may not have been documented.

Through his own observations and personal application and practice of Xuan Kong Flying Stars, Tan was able to spring-clean and remove many of the superfluous parts of the existing literature and texts on Xuan Kong and support the theories with his own case studies. It was Tan, for example, who ascertained that a great deal of Flying Star's Yin House theories were incorrect. Amongst his works that are studied by Classical Feng Shui students extensively are Da San Yuan Xuan Kong Lu Tou 大三元玄空路透 and Da San Yuan Xuan Kong Shi Yan 大三元玄空實驗 (both published in the early 1920s).

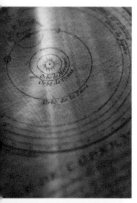

Around the same time Tan did his work on Xuan Kong Flying Stars, there emerged another scholar - Shen Zhu Reng 沈竹仍, a bi-lingual scholar who had both a British and Chinese education. He took a highly intellectual interest in Xuan Kong. Shen broke the mold of writing in the poetic, flowery language and wrote his books on Xuan Kong in plain-speak. He also took the unusual step (at the time) of teaching his knowledge of Xuan Kong publicly to anyone who wanted to learn. Of course today, especially in Hong Kong, this is common. But at the turn of the century, in the Republic Era of China, this was an unusual step.

Shen's book mostly focused on organising, compiling and interpreting Zhang Zhong Shan's works, mainly from the text The Yin and Yang Two House Experiment (陰陽二宅錄驗), into comprehensible language and an easy-to-understand format. He

玄
空
飛
星
風
水

is credited with 'discovering' the Flying Star technique from Zhang's work after studying over a thousand Yi Jing books. Shen also stripped out a lot of the unnecessary theories and concepts, simplifying Xuan Kong Feng Shui and distilling a lot of the ideas into a system we know today as Xuan Kong Flying Stars.

His book - Shen's Xuan Kong Study 沈氏玄空學 (Shen Shi Xuan Kong Xue) published around early 1930s by his son, is one of the key seminal texts on Xuan Kong Flying Stars Feng Shui. His work remains one of the most widely referenced texts on Xuan Kong Flying Stars to date.

If you wish to read a full biography on Shen Zhu Reng, you may logon on to ***www.masteryacademy.com/bio/zhureng***.

玄
空
飛
星
風
水

# The Popularity of Xuan Kong Flying Stars

From the origins story I have just shared with you, you can see that Xuan Kong Flying Stars is a relatively 'new' system in the family of Classical Feng Shui. With Shen's works, Xuan Kong Flying Stars became immediately accessible and it grew in popularity simply because Shen's books simplified the system and boiled it down to some of the bare basics. His willingness to teach Xuan Kong Flying Stars made it easy for anyone to learn Xuan Kong and Feng Shui. His books made Xuan Kong Flying Stars accessible to anyone willing to put in some work to also learn the Flying Stars system.

Xuan Kong Flying Stars remains popular TODAY largely because it is a system of Feng Shui that is highly suited to the demands of modern society. Xuan Kong Flying Stars brings about relatively fast results, and is suited for urban living, particularly for apartments and condominiums. It is also relatively easy to implement, and the computations do not require a great deal of formulas or extremely exacting conditions.

However, Flying Stars is but a small component of Xuan Kong Feng Shui.Beyond Flying Stars, there are other sub-systems like Xuan Kong 64 Hexagram 玄空 大卦 (Xuan Kong Da Gua), Xuan Kong Six Methods 玄空六法 (Xuan Kong Liu Fa), Xuan Kong Purple White Divination 玄空紫白訣 (Xuan Kong Zi Bai Jue) and Xuan Kong Date Selection 玄空擇日 (Xuan Kong Ze Ri). Xuan Kong is an extremely sophisticated system of Feng Shui with many levels and a great deal of depth to its practice.

But it is a great system for individuals of all levels to gain an introduction to Classical Feng Shui, specifically Xuan Kong Feng Shui. And over the course of the next 7 chapters, you will

玄
空
飛
星
風
水

find out just how easy Xuan Kong Flying Stars is to implement and utilise, and why it is such a popular system.

To give you a good grounding and foundation in the basics, I have devoted 2 chapters to the key basic information you will need. These are the bare basics, absolutely essential fundamentals you will need to learn Flying Stars, and for those who intend to advance beyond Flying Stars, to study Xuan Kong Feng Shui.

I will also share with you knowledge about the practical side of Flying Stars, from how to take a direction, to how to plot a Flying Star chart. Then of course, there is the interpretation of the Flying Stars chart, something that many books do not talk about, and more importantly, practical solutions to some of the common problems and conundrums related to Flying Stars. Finally, there is a walk-through examples section in Chapter 8 which will show you how to undertake an audit of a property, using Flying Stars.

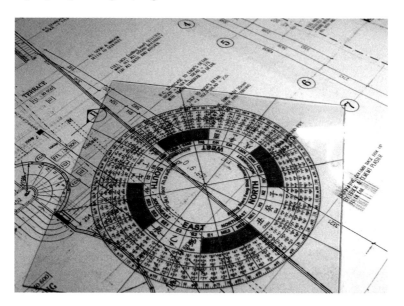

玄空飛星風水

**2**

玄空飛星風水

Chapter 2:
# Feng Shui
# Fundamentals

玄
空
飛
星
風
水

**F**eng Shui is a subject with many layers to it - it is a field of study that has great depth, but yet, great simplicity in its application. Indeed, those of you who have studied BaZi will know that as your appreciation of the subject grows, so your understanding of the basic fundamentals deepens. It is the same with Feng Shui, or for that matter, any subject or field of study! You can memorise and learn all the complex formulas, and may have read all the classics, but as long as there is no mastery of the basics, your understanding and ability to apply what you have learnt or read is limited.

The purpose of this chapter is to expose you to some of the basic underlying principles and fundamental theories behind Feng Shui. As your understanding of Feng Shui and particularly Xuan Kong Flying Stars Feng Shui deepens, you will begin to see how even the most complicated theories are rooted in the principles that you will read about in this chapter.

玄
空
風
水

Those of you who do not read Chinese should not be alarmed. You are not at any particular disadvantage. It is just a matter of learning a little terminology and familiarising yourself with some of the basic terms. In any case, I have provided English translations of the terms here. These are by no means 'universal' translations - different schools may choose to use different English descriptions. But the principles, the bedrock foundation of Feng Shui, remain the same.

玄空飛星風水

After you have finished this book, return to this chapter and re-read it. You will find you have a new understanding of the fundamentals and have gained new insight into the other chapters in this book. Similarly, as you make your way through my *Xuan Kong Feng Shui* series of books, you will find that I will frequently revisit these key principles and your understanding of the Ba Gua, and the application of principles like the Early Heaven and Later Heaven Ba Gua will consequently deepen. Those of you interested in the Yi Jing will also find these basics useful as Yi Jing studies are greatly orientated around the He Tu, the Luo Shu and the Ba Gua.

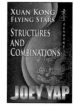

In this chapter, we'll start with the broad over-arching principles first, before drilling down to the hard fundamentals. Don't pooh-pooh the metaphysical and philosophical parts of the discussion - remember, Feng Shui did not begin its origins as a 'great wealth enhancer' or a cure-all for personal problems. It originated as a means of tapping into the natural energies of the universe or environment, for the betterment of life. Understanding the philosophical tenets of Feng Shui is as important as the 'hard fundamentals'.

玄
空
風
水

# First, there was Darkness, then Light

Everyone knows the phrase 'Yin' and 'Yang'. The understanding of Yin and Yang that most people have is not wrong - it is often viewed as a variation of either one positive, one negative, black and white, male and female, and of course, the epitome of the concept of balance and equilibrium. In the study of Feng Shui, and many other Metaphysical studies, Yin and Yang is central to gaining an understanding of the more complex principles and the application of sophisticated theories.

Yin and Yang at its most basic level, refers to two types of energies: moving and unmoving, passive and active. Simplistically, this is represented by two types of lines: a broken line (Yin) and a straight strong line (Yang). Chinese sages then added to this, the concept of duality. Within all Yang, there is Yin. Within all Yin, there is Yang.

陰
*Yin*

陽
*Yang*

A popular modern day phrase that captures well the concept of duality is "opposites attract". Oppositional forces can also be complementary in nature. That which is unknown is defined by that which is known. Many of the common opposites which we know are actually a representation of Yin and Yang. Think of night and day, outside and inside, high and low, forward and backwards, love and hate, positive and negative, real and false, the conscious and the subconscious. So much of our universe is represented in terms of Yin and Yang. For example, all computer programs comprise of a series of 1 and 0 numbers that form binary code. Morse Code comprises of combinations of dots and dashes!

玄
空
飛
星
風
水

What the principle of Yin and Yang is trying to tell us is that nothing exists in absolute form or in itself. It is a part of something. A bit like that famous saying by John Donne: "No man is an island, entire of itself".

The pictorial representation of Yin and Yang can be seen in the above diagram. This pictorial representation captures not only the concept of Yin within Yang, and Yang within Yin, but also a lot of the important ideas that are derived from the basic principle. From this diagram, we can surmise that everything is a cycle and nothing is permanent. We can also say that achieving balance is about Yin and Yang, and not one without the other.

Of course, what I have discussed here about Yin and Yang is very simplistic and basic. I have left out much of the philosophical discussion because it probably would warrant an entire book in itself, and not just a section in a chapter. Furthermore, the objective of introducing you to the theory of Yin and Yang is so that you are able to see its application in Feng Shui, and not to embark on a discussion about Chinese Metaphysics.

玄
空
飛
星
風
水

As you read through this section and the rest of this book, always keep in mind the theory of Yin and Yang. Taoists and ancient sages used the principle of Yin and Yang to explain everything in the universe. And often, you'll find in Feng Shui, that is what we are striving to achieve - balance, equilibrium, harmony, with Yin and Yang in co-existance. Remember what I said about how Feng Shui is about great complexity embedded within great simplicity? Yin and Yang can also be expanded into a tremendously complex philosophy, or a simplistic concept.

You might be wondering: What does Yin and Yang have to do with Feng Shui? Qi is produced by the merging of Yin and Yang in our universe and environment. How do Yin and Yang merge? Through the convergence of Water and Mountain – and yes, I am talking about real water and real mountains.

In Feng Shui, that which is Yin in nature is represented by the Mountains. Remember, Yin is unmoving, or still. Hence it is represented by Mountains – when was the last time you saw a mountain move by itself? By contrast, that which is Yang in nature is represented by Water. Yang is moving and active. Water is a moving substance. Thus is considered Yang.

Mountain and Water. Yin and Yang.

玄
空
飛
星
風
水

On the micro scale, Yin and Yang can be seen in the context of the Internal and External aspects of the House. Inside a house, doors and pathways are Yang, whilst bedrooms are Yin.

The concept of Yin and Yang permeates every aspect of Feng Shui, from the broadest theory, to the most exacting application. In Xuan Kong Flying Stars Feng Shui, even the Stars have Yin and Yang aspects, as represented by their positive and negative attributes.

## The Trigrams

Linked to the concept of Yin and Yang are Trigrams or Guas. This is essentially a set of images, derived from the original representation of Yin and Yang as a broken line (Yin) and a straight line (Yang). Originally, only four images were derived from the permutations of Yin and Yang - these are known as the 4 Images or Si Xiang.

| 陰<br>Yin | | 陽<br>Yang | |
|---|---|---|---|
| ▬ ▬ | | ▬▬▬ | |
| ▬▬ ▬▬ | ▬▬▬ ▬▬ | ▬▬ ▬▬ | ▬▬▬ |
| 太陰<br>Greater Yin | 少陽<br>Lesser Yang | 少陰<br>Lesser Yin | 太陽<br>Greater Yang |

玄空飛星風水

This partly explains why there are so many quad-groupings in Chinese Metaphysical studies. We have the four cardinal directions (North, South, East, West), and the 12 Earthly Branches are grouped in fours, be it by season or by category (Cardinals, Stables or Graveyards).

### Seasonal Grouping

| 寅 | 卯 | 辰 | 巳 | 午 | 未 | 申 | 酉 | 戌 | 亥 | 子 | 丑 |
|---|---|---|---|---|---|---|---|---|---|---|---|
| *Yin* | *Mao* | *Chen* | *Si* | *Wu* | *Wei* | *Shen* | *You* | *Xu* | *Hai* | *Zi* | *Chou* |
| Tiger | Rabbit | Dragon | Snake | Horse | Goat | Monkey | Rooster | Dog | Pig | Rat | Ox |

| 春 Spring | 夏 Summer | 秋 Autumn | 冬 Winter |
|---|---|---|---|

### The 4 Cardinals 四正

| 卯 | 午 | 酉 | 子 |
|---|---|---|---|
| *Mao* | *Wu* | *You* | *Zi* |
| Rabbit | Horse | Rooster | Rat |

### The 4 Growths 四生

| 寅 | 巳 | 申 | 亥 |
|---|---|---|---|
| *Yin* | *Si* | *Shen* | *Hai* |
| Tiger | Snake | Monkey | Pig |

### The 4 Graveyards 四墓

| 辰 | 未 | 戌 | 丑 |
|---|---|---|---|
| *Chen* | *Wei* | *Xu* | *Chou* |
| Dragon | Goat | Dog | Ox |

The Eight Trigrams are as follows:

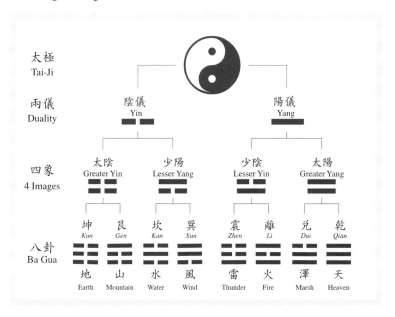

By adding an additional Yin and Yang line to the top of the 4 Images, an additional 4 permutations can be derived. These are known as the 8 Trigrams or Guas.

Each Gua comprises of three lines or three Yao. Therefore, each Gua embraces the concept of the Cosmic Trinity as each Yao line represents Heaven-Man-Earth. Naturally, the top Yao line represents Heaven, the middle Yao line represents Man, and the bottom Yao line represents Earth.

玄
空
飛
星
風
水

Out of the Eight Trigrams, only two are PURE Yin or PURE Yang. The rest have both Yin and Yang attributes, containing either two Yin and one Yang, or one Yin and two Yang, with differing order. However, within the grouping of 8, each Trigram has a Yin or Yang attribute, based on the number of Yin or Yang lines it has. If a Trigram only has one Yin line, it has a Yin attribute. If it has only one Yang line, it has a Yang attribute.

| 坤 Kun | 艮 Gen | 坎 Kan | 巽 Xun | 震 Zhen | 離 Li | 兌 Dui | 乾 Qian |
|---|---|---|---|---|---|---|---|
| ☷ | ☶ | ☵ | ☴ | ☳ | ☲ | ☱ | ☰ |
| 陰 Yin | 陽 Yang | 陽 Yang | 陰 Yin | 陽 Yang | 陰 Yin | 陰 Yin | 陽 Yang |

Using the Trigrams, ancient Chinese sages, like Fu Xi 伏羲, were able to attach a Gua or image to virtually everything known in the universe. The Trigrams were used to represent amongst other things, people, places, objects, parts of the human anatomy and relationships. The tables overleaf, which are based on the classic Shuo Gua Zhuan 說卦傳 tell you a little bit about what each Gua or

*Fu xi 伏羲*

image is associated with. This is not a comprehensive list but simply a brief taster of the power of the Trigrams. The study of the Yi Jing affords a deeper understanding of the Trigrams but is not within the scope of this book. For now, focus on understanding the basic aspects that each Trigram represents.

玄空飛星風水

## 乾 Qian ☰

| | |
|---|---|
| **Element** | Metal |
| **Image** | Heaven |
| **Number** | 6 |
| **People** | Father, senior person, chairman of the company, a leader, a manager, the family breadwinner |
| **Part of the body** | Head, bones, lungs, the mind |
| **Illness** | Brain-related ailments, lung disease, muscle-related ailments |
| **Animal** | Horse, swan, lion, elephant, large animals |
| **Colour** | White, gold, silver |
| **Direction** | Northwest |

玄
空
飛
星
風
水

## 坤 Kun ☷

| | |
|---|---|
| **Element** | Earth |
| **Image** | Earth |
| **Number** | 2 |
| **People** | Mother or motherly figure, old ladies, villagers |
| **Part of the body** | Abdomen, spleen, stomach |
| **Illness** | Stomach disorders, indigestion, abdominal pain |
| **Animal** | Cow, mare |
| **Colour** | Yellow, black |
| **Direction** | Southwest |

玄空飛星風水

## 震 Zhen ☳

| Element | Wood |
|---|---|
| Image | Thunder |
| Number | 3 |
| People | Eldest son, military or polite personnel, sportsmen, a new or emerging leader |
| Part of the body | Feet, liver, hair, larynx |
| Illness | Problems with the feet and legs, liver disease or problems related to the liver, anxiety |
| Animal | Dragon, insects |
| Colour | Dark green, jade green |
| Direction | East |

玄
空
飛
星
風
水

## 巽 Xun ☴

| | |
|---|---|
| **Element** | Wood |
| **Image** | Wind |
| **Number** | 4 |
| **People** | Eldest daughter, first born daughter, a widow |
| **Part of the body** | Upper leg, thigh, buttocks |
| **Illness** | Gastrointestinal problems, arm and thigh sprains, stroke |
| **Animal** | Chickens, jungle animals, snake |
| **Colour** | Green, white, jade green |
| **Direction** | Southeast |

玄空飛星風水

## 坎 Kan ☵

| Element | Water |
|---|---|
| Image | Water |
| Number | 1 |
| People | Middle son, people who work at sea |
| Part of the body | Ear, circulatory system, blood, kidneys |
| Illness | Ear and hearing ailments, kidney disease, diarrhoa, circulation problem |
| Animal | Pigs, fish and animals that live in the sea |
| Colour | Black |
| Direction | North |

玄
空
飛
星
風
水

## 離 Li ☲

| | |
|---|---|
| **Element** | Fire |
| **Image** | Fire |
| **Number** | 9 |
| **People** | Middle daughter, creative persons, military personnel |
| **Part of the body** | Eyes and heart |
| **Illness** | Vision-related problems (cataracts, detached retina), cardiac disease or cardiac problems |
| **Animal** | Wild birds and fowl, tortoises, crustaceans |
| **Colour** | Red |
| **Direction** | South |

玄
空
飛
星
風
水

## 艮 Gen ☶

| | |
|---|---|
| **Element** | Earth |
| **Image** | Mountain |
| **Number** | 8 |
| **People** | Young children, hermits |
| **Part of the body** | Fingers and toes, the nose, the back and the vertabrae |
| **Illness** | Injuries to fingers and toes |
| **Animal** | Tiger, cats, dogs |
| **Colour** | Yellow |
| **Direction** | Northeast |

玄
空
飛
星
風
水

## 兌 Dui ☱

| | |
|---|---|
| **Element** | Metal |
| **Image** | Marsh |
| **Number** | 7 |
| **People** | Youngest daughter, young female, singers and actors, people who make a living using communicative skills |
| **Part of the body** | Mouth, tongue and throat |
| **Illness** | Oral disease, problems with the tongue, ulcers, respiratory ailments |
| **Animal** | Swamp animals |
| **Colour** | White |
| **Direction** | West |

玄
空
飛
星
風
水

# The Power of 3

Another very important Metaphysical concept that permeates through Feng Shui and other fields like Yi Jing 易經, BaZi 八字 (Four Pillars of Destiny), Zi Wei 紫微 and Mian Xiang 面相 (Face Reading) is that of the Cosmic Trinity.

The concept of the Cosmic Trinity is that all things in life and the universe can be defined and ordered, using the principle of Heaven-Earth-Man. The typical application of the Cosmic Trinity is in the concept of a person's success. In Chinese Metaphysics, a person's potential in life can be determined by looking at their Heaven Luck (their BaZi or Astrology), their Earth Luck (their Feng Shui) and their Man Luck (their personal efforts).

The Cosmic Trinity, like Yin and Yang, is a broad concept that permeates through all levels of Classical Feng Shui, so keep it at the forefront as you begin to gain a greater understanding of Feng Shui.

玄
空
飛
星
風
水

# The Five Elements

If you have studied BaZi, you will have some familiarity with the Five Elements cycle or Wu Xing 五行. The term 'Wu Xing' can loosely be translated to Five Transformations or Five Phases, but today, we often use the short-hand of 'Five Elements'.

The Five Elements are derivatives of the theory of Yin and Yang and also, from the understanding of the universe and cosmos, as well as the flow and movement of energy that the Chinese sages derived from the He Tu, which I will talk about in a little while.

While there is some argument that the Five Elements theory is derived from the observation of nature, it is more precise to say it originated from the theories on the phases of energy or Qi and their cyclical and Yin and Yang patterns. Accordingly, we are interested in how these five types of energies interact with each other when we study the Five Elements. This is not to say that the observations that co-relate with nature and the universe are wrong or not relevant - rather, the origins of the Five Elements theory is not so much from the actual observation of nature, as much as it is from the He Tu or River Map.

The Western science of physics (in particular, thermodynamics and electromagnetism) is probably the closest approximation of the study of the Five Elements. Both are concerned with understanding the way energy transforms and changes. The difference is that Five Elements theory continues to maintain a Metaphysical side to its application whilst physics has abandoned its natural science origins.

玄空飛星風水

The Five Elements theory is an important basic piece of knowledge that you must grasp thoroughly. At every level of Classical Feng Shui and BaZi, we return to the Five Elements and delve deeper into its workings and theories. However, as this is a beginner's book, what you simply need to know at this point are the bare basics. And the bare basics of the theory are as simple as knowing the Five Elements and understanding the three cycles of the Five Elements: the Production Cycle, the Controlling Cycle and the Weakening Cycle.

The Five Elements are as follows:

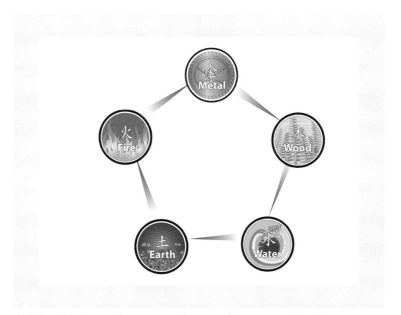

Whilst the Five Elements relate to five particular elements, it is important to remember that they also represent five phases or transformations of energy and can also simply represent five types of energy.

In addition to knowing the Five Elements, we must also know how these elements interact and how the energies alter and change between the Five Elements. Hence, we must understand the three cycles.

玄
空
飛
星
風
水

## The Productive Cycle 生

The Productive Cycle, or Xiang Sheng, is a positive transformation of the energies and is sometimes known as the forward cycle. In this cycle, the Five Elements interact harmoniously with each other and grow and expand the energies within.

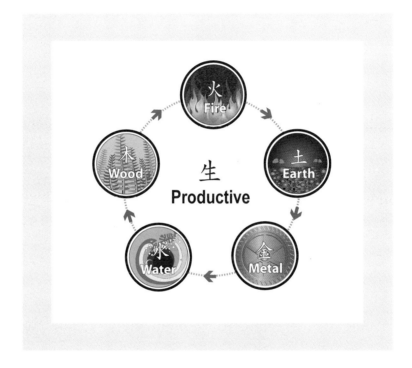

In the Productive Cycle, Wood creates Fire and Fire in turn burns substance into ash, producing Earth. From the Earth comes Metal, in the form of minerals. Metal, through condensation, attracts Water, which in turn, nourishes and grows Wood.

玄
空
飛
星
風
水

**The Controlling Cycle** 剋

The Controlling Cycle involves the use of aggressive and oppositional force of one element to control another element.

In the Controlling Cycle, Water extinguishes or 'controls' Fire. Fire in turn, melts or 'controls' Metal. Metal cuts Wood, thus it 'controls' Wood. Wood in the form of the roots of plants can break the Earth, and thus Wood 'controls' Earth. Earth meanwhile is what borders and holds in Water, thus, Water is controlled by Earth.

玄
空
飛
星
風
水

## The Weakening Cycle 洩

The Weakening Cycle involves an element draining the energies of the element that produces it. This transformation is not a forceful or aggressive process, but rather, is a natural use of the manner in which the energies transform between phases.

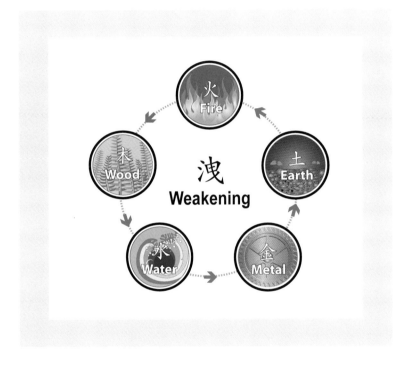

In the Weakening Cycle, Wood is nourished by Water. Thus Wood weakens Water. Metal is weakened by Water because Metal produces water. Earth must be broken up and mined to produce minerals (Metal), thus in the process Earth is weakened. So, Metal weakens Earth. Fire produces earth, but too much Earth will put out the Fire. Finally, Wood is burnt to make Fire thus Fire weakens Wood.

玄
空
飛
星
風
水

It is important not to place any bias or prejudice on the three cycles. Remember, in Feng Shui, everything has a purpose and every theory has an application and a use. A Weakening Cycle has its uses, and there are times when we want to use a Controlling Cycle. Try to commit the three cycles to memory as it will help with your understanding of the application of many theories in Feng Shui.

The philosophical and 'origins' arguments about many of these basic concepts can go on and on, so we sometimes have to cut to the chase (or cut the crap, as I tell my students) and figure out what is important and what can be saved for teahouse conversation. What is important at this stage is that you understand that the broad over-arching theories and philosophies are all inter-connected and that Yin and Yang, the Cosmic Trinity and the Five Element theory are an essential part of your understanding of Feng Shui.

Now that we have the broad concepts in hand, it's time to move on to the hard fundamentals of Feng Shui.

玄
空
飛
星
風
水

# The He Tu, Luo Shu and Ba Gua:
# The Foundations of Feng Shui

Every 'Feng Shui Fundamentals' discussion must, by necessity, begin with a conversation about the He Tu 河圖 and Luo Shu 洛書. These are two models with numerical, directional, combinational and divinatory significance that are what almost every Feng Shui (and also Yi Jing) application comes back to. If we were to use the computer program analogy, the He Tu and the Luo Shu, are the original code of the program. Everything else is an evolution, or an additional build, on top of this basic original code.

According to legend, the He Tu and Luo Shu were derived from sightings of two unique creatures, during the era of the sage Fu Xi (approximately 2800BC) in China. The first creature, a dragon-headed Horse with carp-like scales, was spotted at the Yellow River. Its body contained unique and strange markings which were noted by the sages and then studied in depth. After much detailed study of the markings, the sages concluded that the markings on the horse could be arranged into a model of dots. This model was named the He Tu or River Map.

玄空飛星風水

Further study of the He Tu, coupled with their own observations of nature and their surroundings, enabled the ancient Chinese sages to derive certain understandings about the planet and universe, which only became accepted facts centuries later, when man began to circumvent the earth and discover

*The He Tu*

new lands as well as advance scientifically. For example, the North-South axis of the Earth was derived from the He Tu by Chinese sages. Modern science tells us that magnetic energies of the Earth travel from the South to the North! Similarly, the principle that heat rises to the top, whilst cool energies flow to the bottom was discerned by the ancient Chinese sages from the He Tu. This is a basic scientific principle that almost everyone knows today.

Through the simple He Tu diagram, the Chinese sages derived much understanding about the universe that we take for granted today. Through the times, the He Tu model was refined and given an additional layer of context: directional and elemental context. The sages noticed the Southern sections of their country were warmer. Similarly, the sages noticed vegetation in the East blossomed but was less prominent in the rocky mountains of the West.

Thus, as heat rises to the top, and the South was where the climate was warmer, the ancient sages concluded that Fire and the South direction, formed the top part of the He Tu. And since energies moved downwards from the top to the bottom, they fixed the North at the bottom, and concluded that it was 'Water' in nature since water flows downwards. As the East was where all the vegetation and fruit grew, it was viewed as elementally associated with Wood. All of China's minerals came from the West, so that direction was given the attribute of Metal.

If you look at the dot model of the He Tu, you will notice a few things. Each dot is equivalent to a number, based on the number of dots in each row. Notice how 1 and 6 are at the bottom, 2 and 7 are at the top, 3 and 8 are on the left and 4 and 9 are on the right?

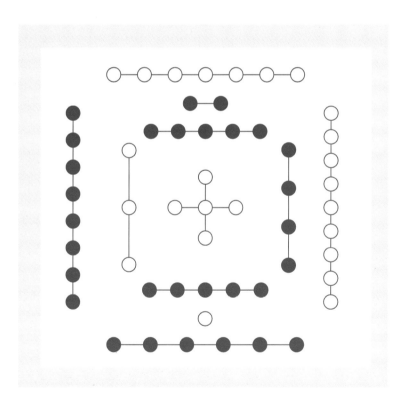

So, when we put the numerical information, together with the directional and elemental information, we get this diagram:

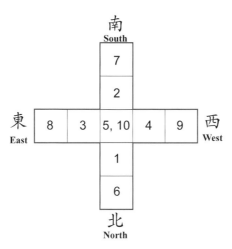

*The He Tu*

And from this diagram, we can draw the following conclusions:

- 2 and 7 are at the South and both have Fire attributes
- 1 and 6 are at the North and both have Water attributes
- 3 and 8 are at the East and both have Wood attributes
- 4 and 9 are at the West and both have Metal attributes
- 5 and 10 are at the center, and have Earth attributes.

玄
空
飛
星
風
水

The dot model of the He Tu also incorporates the theory of Yin and Yang, as well as the Cosmic Trinity. Notice how 1 opposes 2, and the dot model's Yin and Yang markings mirror that of the Yin and Yang diagram earlier? You may also have noticed that the black dots all comprise of even numbers and are all Yin, whilst the white dots are all odd numbers and are all Yang in nature. Odd Yang numbers are located on the top end or Heaven, even numbers with Yin are on Earth.

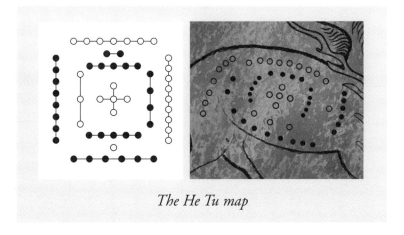

*The He Tu map*

From this dot model alone, many numerical combinations, Five Element and Yin and Yang applications can be derived. In fact, two well known classical texts, 'He Luo Li Shu' 河洛理數 and 'Shuo Gua Chuan' 說卦傳 are devoted entirely on this subject matter. These are of course very sophisticated ideas and not appropriate for a beginner's text - we will revisit the He Tu again as we delve deeper into Xuan Kong Feng Shui.

For now, focus on understanding and remembering which numbers associate with which directions (North, South, East, West) and also which numbers associate with which Elements (Fire, Water, Earth, Wood, Metal) and finally, which numbers are Yin and which are Yang.

玄空飛星風水

# The Ba Gua

From the He Tu, the ancient Sages, in particular, Fu Xi, added the Trigrams, to derive a model of the universe that is known as the Ba Gua. Now, this is not a reference to the eight sided mirror that many people associate with the term 'Ba Gua'. That is a Ba Gua mirror - it is not the same as the Ba Gua model that we are looking at here.

The Ba Gua is a mathematical model that takes the He Tu and merges and synergises it with the Trigrams. It is essentially a harmonisation of several different ideas: Yin and Yang, the Cosmic Trinity, the Trigrams, and some of the elemental information derived from the He Tu.

The first Ba Gua the sage Fu Xi conceptualised was a square map, with the information aligned in a linear form.

| Original Number | | 1 | 2 | 3 | 4 | 5 | 6 | 7 | 8 |
|---|---|---|---|---|---|---|---|---|---|
| 八卦 8 Gua | **Name** | 乾 *Qian* | 兌 *Dui* | 離 *Li* | 震 *Zhen* | 巽 *Xun* | 坎 *Kan* | 艮 *Gen* | 坤 *Kun* |
| | **Image** | ☰ | ☱ | ☲ | ☳ | ☴ | ☵ | ☶ | ☷ |
| 四象 **4 Images** | | 太陽 Greater Yang | | 少陰 Lesser Yin | | 少陽 Lesser Yang | | 太陰 Greater Yin | |
| 兩儀 **Duality** | | 陽 Yang | | | | 陰 Yin | | | |
| 太極 **Tai-Ji** | | ☯ | | | | | | | |

玄
空
飛
星
風
水

This was then further tweaked and adjusted ingeniously, to become what is essentially a square map, but presented in a round form! (remember, Yin and Yang?) This created an ideal model of the universe - it maintained the concept of directions, but yet being round, was an infinite loop, representing the endless nature of the universe and cosmos. Many of the ideas in the Ba Gua model combine dualistic ideas: a fixed number of seasons (4) with an infinite number of cycles of the seasons. There are Four Cardinal directions, but these directions have no fixed start and end point.

Fu Xi's Ba Gua became known as the Early Heaven Ba Gua. In the Early Heaven Ba Gua, the Trigram Qian is located on top, to symbolise Heaven above and Kun at the bottom to symbolise the Earth below. South is Qian because it is strong and extreme Yang, and also, represents highly mobile energies. This arrangement also seems to be in line with the magnetic fields on the planet which flow from South to the North.

The Early Heaven Ba Gua 先天八卦 (Xian Tian Ba Gua) represents a fixed view of the universe. In this model, the patterns, be it numerical, directional or elemental, are fixed and unchanging. It symbolises the perfect, the ideal. It is a depiction of the cosmos as it should be.

玄
空
飛
星
風
水

## The Ba Gua evolves!

According to legend, in the era of Xia Yu (夏禹), a giant turtle with black and white spots on its shell was found beside the River Luo. The turtle had a distinct appearance that had never before been seen. Recalling the tale of the dragon-headed Horse that had also risen from the river with markings on its back, ancient Chinese sages immediately connected the two and compared the markings.

Luo Shu

The markings on the turtle's back were similar in presentation to those derived by the sages into the form of the dot model of the He Tu. The difference is the numbers and the directions were more clearly presented. On the turtle's back were 9 dots at the South, 1 dot at the North, 3 dots at the East, 7 dots at the West, 4 dots at the Southeast, 8 dots at the Northeast, 2 dots at the Southwest, and 6 dots at the Northwest.

玄
空
飛
星
風
水

From here, the ancient Chinese sages derived what is known today as the Luo Shu 洛書 or Luo Book. It is essentially a group of numbers, arranged on a 9 box grid.

*The Luo Shu Square*

Using the information derived from the Luo Shu, the Ba Gua model derived by Fu Xi was re-visited by the famous philosopher-King of the Zhou Dynasty, King Wen (Wen Wang). The Wen Wang Ba Gua later became known as the Later Heaven Ba Gua 後天八卦 (Hou Tian Ba Gua). The Later Heaven Ba Gua takes into account the imperfections and chaos in the universe, and places the Trigrams in a manner that takes into account fluctuations and changes in energy flow and patterns. The Trigrams were also re-arranged to synergise information about the eight directions and the seasons of nature.

玄空飛星風水

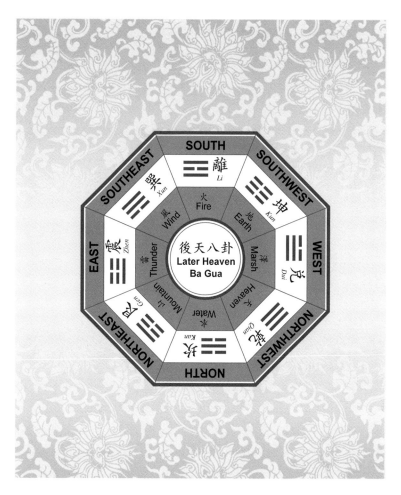

For example, in the Early Heaven Ba Gua, Li is on the left, and Qian is on top. But in the Later Heaven Ba Gua, Li is on top because King Wen rationalised, Fire burns bright and has rising energies, thus it should be located at the top. Similarly, Water when poured onto the ground moved downwards, even as it seeped through the earth. So he placed Kan at the bottom. Similarly, as the sun rises in the East, it is appropriate for Zhen to be in that direction, since the imagery of Zhen is that of the light breaking the darkness. The setting sun casts a shadow over the sky, similar to the imagery of the trigram Dui, thus Dui came to occupy the West direction.

玄空飛星風水

In the application of Feng Shui, both the Early Heaven and Later Heaven models are used in tandem. Since the Early Heaven Ba Gua represents the ideal and the perfect, the unchanging and fixed, it is simply a matter of Yin and Yang, that there must also be a model that represents the now, the current, the changing, which is the Later Heaven Ba Gua. The Later Heaven Ba Gua considers and takes into account variations and changes and so can be said to represent the application of the theory of the Early Heaven Ba Gua.

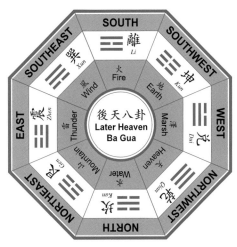

玄
空
飛
星
風
水

# Ba Gua Boggling?

The fundamentals I have talked about in this Chapter are essential in order to enable you to understand the WHY behind Xuan Kong Feng Shui and Xuan Kong Flying Stars. Once you have understood the reasoning and the concepts behind Feng Shui, it is easy for you not only to apply your knowledge to different situations, but also be able to comprehend how to 'think' your way out of a Feng Shui problem, especially when there are conflicting theories or ideas and reconciling them appears impossible.

At this point, it's possible that some of you may find the information a little overwhelming and are uncertain as to what you should focus your attention. In between all the philosophical discussions, and the numbers, directions, elements and models, it is easy to get lost. So, I'm going to boil things down to the absolute necessity that you should have grasped and should keep in mind.

玄空飛星風水

**Who's Who?** You need to be able to tell the He Tu and Luo Shu apart, based on their configuration. The He Tu has numbers arranged like a cross, whilst the Luo Shu is arranged according to a 9 Grid.

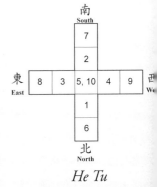

*He Tu*

**Numbers Game:** You need to know which numbers in the He Tu are grouped together. For example, 1 and 6 are grouped together in the He Tu, as are 3 and 8, 4 and 9, 5 and 10. You need to know which number goes into which Grid on the Luo Shu.

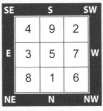

*Luo Shu*

**Elements:** You need to be able to recognise which numbers are associated with which elements. For example, 1-6 = Water, 2-7 =Fire, 3-8 = Wood and 4-9 = Metal.

**Who's Your Ba Gua:** You need to be able to tell the Early Heaven Ba Gua and Later Heaven Ba Gua apart. Tip: look at the position of Li and Kan Trigrams.

**Elements, Directions and Numbers:** You need to know which numbers are associated which directions, Trigrams and elements, in the Later Heaven Ba Gua.

It's a lot to remember and I don't expect you to be able to commit all these to memory right away. So dog-ear this chapter and keep referring back to these fundamentals as you work your way through this book.

NB:

*Chapter 2*

# Chapter 3:
# Time, Qi and
# Feng Shui

玄
空
飛
星
風
水

You might be wondering: why is there an entire chapter devoted to Time? Why is Time such an important concept? And what does it have to do with Feng Shui?

In Classical Feng Shui, positive Qi is not everlasting. It is not forever. No building or location has permanent bad luck or permanent good luck. This is why certain areas suddenly boom during certain times, and then experience a downturn during other periods.

In Classical Feng Shui, there are cycles of Qi - upturns and downturns, periods of turmoil and periods of stability. Hence, in almost every Classical Feng Shui system, including Xuan Kong Flying Stars, time is of the essence. Being able to calculate and determine which point of time co-relates to which periods or cycles of energy is an integral part of Classical Feng Shui practice.

Time therefore, in the context of Feng Shui, is a sort of short-hand for the kind of energies prevailing during a point in time, as determined by the energy cycles.

Different schools of Classical Feng Shui each have their own concept of calculating time, but on the fundamentals, notably, the basic Qi cycle, there is little diversion. This is why in the evaluation of the Feng Shui of any property, we must not just consider the environment, the building and the residents, but we must also take into account the factor of Time. Hence, an entire chapter devoted to the concept of Time, in Feng Shui.

玄
空
飛
星
風
水

# Calculating Time

The basis of the computation of time in Feng Shui is very much rooted in astronomy and astrology. The cycles of energy and the passing of time, was referenced against the stars in the sky and the alignment of the planets. The planets Mercury, Venus, Mars, Saturn and Jupiter can actually be viewed with the naked eye from Earth. Indeed, it is believed the planet Jupiter 歲星 (Sui Xing) has a rather big role in many Chinese Metaphysical theories. Many important theories in Feng Shui such as the Grand Duke and Three Killings, are linked to the influence of Jupiter upon the magnetic fields on our planet.

Based on the observations and calculations of Chinese scholars that have been documented since 2500 BC, every 180 years there is a capital transformation of Qi. Why exactly did the Chinese chose 180 years is not clear but is does seem to be related to the three cycles of the Sixty Jia Zi calendar. It is possible that this determination is linked to what is termed 'the Jupiter effect', when all the planets in the solar system align in a straight line, in particular Jupiter and Saturn. However, there is no historical documentation to suggest this is the definitive reason why the Chinese demarcated time this way.

玄
空
飛
星
風
水

# Xuan Kong Feng Shui and the Three Cycles

Xuan Kong Feng Shui, which encompasses Flying Stars, is part of the San Yuan school of Feng Shui. The term 'San Yuan 三元' can be directly translated to 'Three Cycles'. San Yuan's opposite number is the San He school or the 'Three Harmony' school.

The focus of San Yuan Feng Shui systems is heavily orientated around the calculation of the quality and characteristics of Qi in a particular period of time. San He on the other hand, prioritises the observation of natural environmental formations, or Landforms, as it is known.

The name 'San Yuan' tells us that Xuan Kong Flying Stars operates on the idea of 3 cycles of time. Each of these three cycles spans 60 years so 3 cycles = 180 years. Within the 60 years, there are also 3 cycles, each divided into 20 years, known as Periods. Accordingly, each Cycle has 3 Periods. The periods in turn, are governed by a ruling Trigram or Gua. And if you remember, each Gua comprises of 3 Yao. Remember what I said earlier about the Power of 3 in Chinese Metaphysics?

玄空飛星風水

Accordingly, San Yuan Feng Shui takes the view that there is a capital change and transformation in the energies influencing our environment and universe every 20 years.

By understanding the Qi of the Period (also known as the Period Luck 元運), and examining the Qi map for a particular property, a Feng Shui practitioner can ascertain whether or not the property is tapping into positive energies or negative energies.

The diagram below tells us the ruling Trigram for each of the 9 Periods and includes a computation of the years of each Period. Period 5 does not have a ruling Trigram because it is right in the center, and if you look at the original Ba Gua, there is no Trigram that represents the center.

| Cycle 元 | Period 運 | Year 年 | Gua 卦 |
|---|---|---|---|
| 上 Upper | 1 | 1864 - 1883 | ☵ 坎 Kan |
| | 2 | 1884 - 1903 | ☷ 坤 Kun |
| | 3 | 1904 - 1923 | ☳ 震 Zhen |
| 中 Middle | 4 | 1924 - 1943 | ☴ 巽 Xun |
| | 5 | 1944 - 1963 | - |
| | 6 | 1964 - 1983 | ☰ 乾 Qian |
| 下 Lower | 7 | 1984 - 2003 | ☱ 兌 Dui |
| | 8 | 2004 - 2023 | ☶ 艮 Gen |
| | 9 | 2024 - 2043 | ☲ 離 Li |

玄
空
飛
星
風
水

# Tapping into the right Qi

The reason why Xuan Kong places a great deal of emphasis on computing the time factor is because Qi has different qualities, at different points in time. The concept behind Xuan Kong Flying Stars Feng Shui is to compute or calculate the quality of the Qi in a particular property, then tap into the right kind of Qi, while avoiding negative or unfavourable Qi.

The computation of the quality of Qi at any particular period in time, also requires an understanding of the different qualities of Qi. Qi, can have 5 different phases, each with different qualities, vibrancy and potency. The table below shows you the 5 phases of Qi.

| 旺氣<br>*Wang Qi*<br>**Prosperous Qi** | This is the most 'vibrant' form of Qi. Qi in this form is at its optimal stage where it is strong, nurturing and fortunate. It helps accelerates performance and improves the quality of our lives. |
|---|---|
| 生氣<br>*Sheng Qi*<br>**Growing Qi** | Qi in this stage is life-generating and growing. It is strong and promotes prosperity and good fortune. It hastens opportunities and progress. It sharpens our thinking and stabilizes our emotions. |
| 退氣<br>*Tui Qi*<br>**Retreating Qi** | In this stage, the Qi has just expired and is in its waning stage. It is old and beginning to lose its strength. This energy is weakening. |
| 死氣<br>*Si Qi*<br>**Dead Qi** | Qi in this stage is dead and non-moving. These energies can be toxic and obstructing. Qi in this form impedes performance and upsets the balance. This is a stagnant stage of Qi. |
| 煞氣<br>*Sha Qi*<br>**Killing Qi** | This form of Qi is destructive and harmful. Its force is strong yet menacing. Killing Qi reduces vitality and has a blinding effect to one's thinking or performance. This is a violent stage of Qi. |

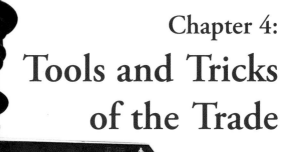

# Chapter 4:
# Tools and Tricks
# of the Trade

玄
空
飛
星
風
水

In the last two chapters, I have shared with you the key basic theories and fundamentals that you need to be able to practice Xuan Kong Flying Stars Feng Shui. Now, you're ready to get your hands dirty with the practical aspects of Flying Star Feng Shui.

The practical aspect of Flying Stars Feng Shui involves two skills: Firstly, the use of the Luo Pan, which is a Feng Shui compass, to establish the direction of a property and secondly, plotting the Flying Stars chart of the property, based on the Facing direction of the property.

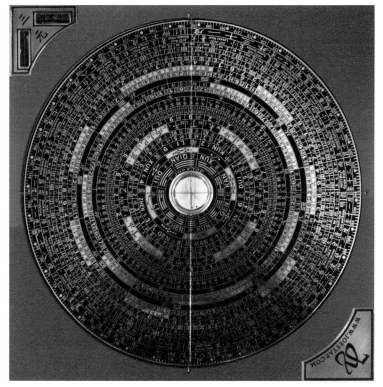

*A San Yuan Luo Pan*

玄
空
飛
星
風
水

Now, taking a direction may seem to be a very simple thing – I'm sure most of you are thinking: How hard is it to stand in front of a building and hold up a Luo Pan, right? But from experience, I can tell you that it is not something that is easy for students to master because sometimes, a building simply does not present an obvious facing. Also, magnetic fields in the building (from metal doors for example) can cause the Luo Pan needle to be unstable or fluctuate.

Thus, taking a direction is therefore as much about judgment as it is about experience, such as knowing where to stand to take a direction and knowing how to handle the situation when there are magnetic fields interfering with a reading. You also need to learn how to 'read' the Luo Pan – at a beginner's level, you may just be interested in the basic direction but as you advance in your study of Feng Shui, you will find the Luo Pan can be used to read a variety of information, beyond just the direction.

## To Luo Pan or not to Luo Pan?

Many beginners and newcomers to Feng Shui are often uncertain as to whether or not they should go the distance and purchase a Luo Pan. What if you are simply interested in doing your own Feng Shui but not anyone else's? You only need to take the direction once surely? So is there the need to go out and buy a Luo Pan? Besides, isn't the Luo Pan just a glorified compass? Let me address some of these concerns here.

First, the Luo Pan is an essential piece of equipment for any Feng Shui enthusiast – after all, who plays

玄
空
飛
星
風
水

tennis without a racquet or golf without a golf set, right? Sure you can borrow one but there's nothing quite like having your own. Secondly, while the basis of the Luo Pan is a compass, a proper Luo Pan doesn't just contain the basic compass, but also includes certain rings around it, with various markings such as the 24 Mountains, 72 Dragons, 64 Hexagrams, Great Sun Formula and 28 Constellations, to name a few.

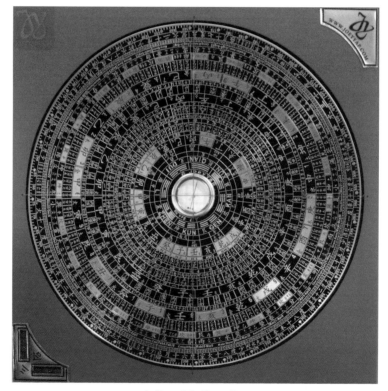

*A San He Luo Pan*

Having these rings and learning how to use them is essential if you intend to go beyond Flying Stars or if you want to use more advanced formulas and theories in Xuan Kong Feng Shui.

玄空飛星風水

Thirdly, while the direction of a property only needs to be taken once to ascertain its Facing Direction to plot the Flying Stars chart, you will find that you also need the Luo Pan for the internal placement of beds and tables, as well as to check the stove mouth direction, when it comes to applying Feng Shui internally.

Typically, a Feng Shui practitioner will have up to 3 types of Luo Pan: a San Yuan Luo Pan, a San He Luo Pan and a Zhong He Luo Pan, which is a combination of the San He-San Yuan Luo Pan. As the focus of this book is Xuan Kong Feng Shui, which is a sub-system of the San Yuan system, only the basic San Yuan Luo Pan rings will be referenced. So if you intend to buy a Luo Pan, you will only need one with the San Yuan rings, specifically the San Yuan 24 Mountain ring.

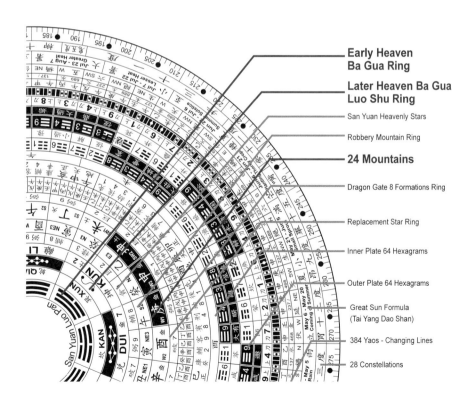

**Early Heaven Ba Gua Ring**

**Later Heaven Ba Gua Luo Shu Ring**

San Yuan Heavenly Stars

Robbery Mountain Ring

**24 Mountains**

Dragon Gate 8 Formations Ring

Replacement Star Ring

Inner Plate 64 Hexagrams

Outer Plate 64 Hexagrams

Great Sun Formula (Tai Yang Dao Shan)

384 Yaos - Changing Lines

28 Constellations

玄
空
飛
星
風
水

Fortunately, there are many semi-professional options available these days for Feng Shui enthusiasts who don't want to go the whole hog with buying equipment. These days, Luo Pans come in many permutations so you don't actually have to buy a 'pro' Luo Pan with all the rings.

However, if you want to make life a little bit easier for yourself, shop around or look around for a Luo Pan that has not only the 24 Mountains Ring, but also the Early Heaven and Later Heaven Ba Gua, along with the Trigrams, located on the Luo Pan's rings. This may seem like nothing more than a bell and whistle added to the basic compass features of the Luo Pan but it does make life easier because then you don't have to keep referring to Chapter 2 or your notes, to know the Trigrams or to check the Ba Guas.

*A Simplified Feng Shui Luo Pan*

玄
空
飛
星
風
水

Although I have in my previous book, ***Feng Shui for Homebuyers - Exterior***, indicated that the use of a scout's compass is sufficient for the purposes of taking a direction, for Flying Stars Feng Shui, you do need a compass that has the 24 Mountains rings.

If you want to use a basic compass, go for a Sunto Compass. This is a very accurate professional compass that gives you very exacting readings on the direction. You then just have to compare the directional degrees of the compass against the 24 Mountains directions to obtain a direction. This is of course quite tiresome and tedious, requiring double work but is a good half-way house option for those who are not comfortable with using a Luo Pan.

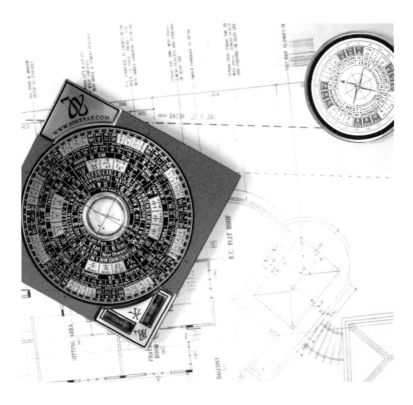

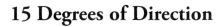
玄
空
飛
星
風
水

# 15 Degrees of Direction

In Feng Shui, direction is an extremely important consideration and factor in determining the quality of Qi in a property or location. At its highest level, and in the application of Feng Shui systems like Dragon-Gate Eight Formations, Xuan Kong Da Gua 64 Hexagrams and 28 Constellations, precision of placement and measurement is crucial to the success of the formulas. So exacting is the formula that it comes down to the exact degree.

At the beginner's level, you don't have to be quite so exacting (although precision is an important part of Feng Shui, especially when it comes to ascertaining directions). However, you do have to be aware that in Feng Shui, the basic directions of North, South, East and West (also known as the Cardinal Directions) can be further bisected into eight directions: North, Northeast, East, Southeast, South, Southwest, West and Northwest.

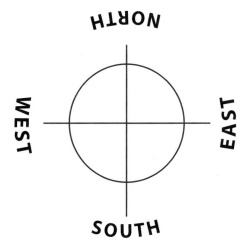

*The 4 Basic directions*

玄空飛星風水

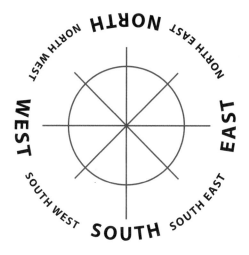

*The 8 main directions*

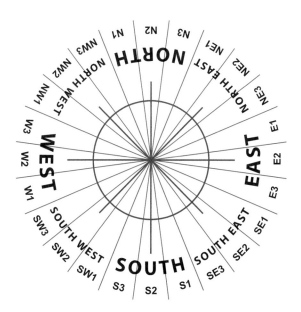

*The 24 directions*

玄空飛星風水

*The 24 Mountain Ring*

The eight directions in turn, can be further trisected into three different directions. Remember the Power of 3? Each of the eight directions is governed by a Trigram. Therefore each direction can be further divided by 3, producing a total of 24 directions. These are known as the 24 Mountains 二十四 山 (Er Shi Si Shan). Accordingly, the South direction can be further divided into South 1 丙, (Bing), South 2 午 (Wu) or South 3 丁 (Ding).

玄
空
飛
星
風
水

The diagram below shows you the three sub-directions, under each of the 8 main directions and the degrees of the Luo Pan or compass that each direction corresponds with.

| Gua | Direction | | Degrees |
|---|---|---|---|
| 離 Li ☲ | South | S1 | 157.6 - 172.5 |
| | | S2 | 172.6 - 187.5 |
| | | S3 | 187.6 -202.5 |
| 坤 Kun ☷ | Southwest | SW1 | 202.6 - 217.5 |
| | | SW2 | 217.6 - 232.5 |
| | | SW3 | 232.6 - 247.5 |
| 兌 Dui ☱ | West | W1 | 247.6 - 262.5 |
| | | W2 | 262.6 - 277.5 |
| | | W3 | 277.6 - 292.5 |
| 乾 Qian ☰ | Northwest | NW1 | 292.6 - 307.5 |
| | | NW2 | 307.6 - 322.5 |
| | | NW3 | 322.6 - 337.5 |
| 坎 Kan ☵ | North | N1 | 337.6 - 352.5 |
| | | N2 | 352.6 - 7.5 |
| | | N3 | 7.6 - 22.5 |
| 艮 Gen ☶ | Northeast | NE1 | 22.6 - 37.5 |
| | | NE2 | 37.6 - 52.5 |
| | | NE3 | 52.6 - 67.5 |
| 震 Zhen ☳ | East | E1 | 67.6 - 82.5 |
| | | E2 | 82.6 - 97.5 |
| | | E3 | 97.6 - 112.5 |
| 巽 Xun ☴ | Southeast | SE1 | 112.6 - 127.5 |
| | | SE2 | 127.6 -142.5 |
| | | SE3 | 142.6 - 157.5 |

玄
空
飛
星
風
水

On the Luo Pan, this is how the 24 Mountains look like:

In my beginners Feng Shui classes, we typically use a little short-hand so the directions are usually written with just the first capital letter and the number. So South 1 would be S1 and Northwest 3 would be NW3. Of course, I always encourage students to eventually master the directions in their original Chinese terms. Thus, a property with a South 1 Facing is referred to as facing Bing 丙, a mountain in South 2 would be referred to as a mountain at Wu 午 and water at South 3 would be referred to as Water coming in at Ding 丁.

玄
空
飛
星
風
水

It is important also at this point that you are aware of the Yin and Yang qualities of each of the 24 Mountains. Each basic direction comprises of either one Yang and two Yin sub-directions, or two Yin and one Yang sub-directions. For shorthand, they have been expressed in the form of (-) for Yin, and (+) for Yang in this diagram.

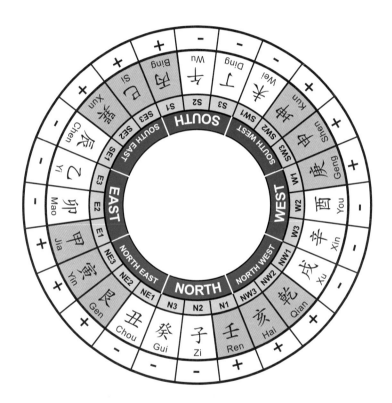

So, if you look at the Northwest direction, you can see that Northwest 1 is Yin, whilst Northwest 2 and 3 are Yang. In the South, South 1 is Yang, whilst South 2 and 3 are Yin.

玄空飛星風水

The table below provides a quick reference guide for all the relevant information on the 24 Mountains, including the respective degrees and polarity (Yin / Yang).

| Gua | Direction | 24 Mountains | | | | Polarity | Degrees |
|---|---|---|---|---|---|---|---|
| 離 Li | South | S1 | 丙 | Bing | Yang Fire | + | 157.6 - 172.5 |
| | | S2 | 午 | Wu | Horse (Yang Fire) | - | 172.6 - 187.5 |
| | | S3 | 丁 | Ding | Yin Fire | - | 187.6 -202.5 |
| 坤 Kun | Southwest | SW1 | 未 | Wei | Goat (Yin Earth) | - | 202.6 - 217.5 |
| | | SW2 | 坤 | Kun | Southwest (Earth) | + | 217.6 - 232.5 |
| | | SW3 | 申 | Shen | Monkey (Yang Metal) | + | 232.6 - 247.5 |
| 兌 Dui | West | W1 | 庚 | Geng | Yang Metal | + | 247.6 - 262.5 |
| | | W2 | 酉 | You | Rooster (Yin Metal) | - | 262.6 - 277.5 |
| | | W3 | 辛 | Xin | Yin Metal | - | 277.6 - 292.5 |
| 乾 Qian | Northwest | NW1 | 戌 | Xu | Dog (Yang Earth) | - | 292.6 - 307.5 |
| | | NW2 | 乾 | Qian | Northwest (Metal) | + | 307.6 - 322.5 |
| | | NW3 | 亥 | Hai | Pig (Yin Water) | + | 322.6 - 337.5 |
| 坎 Kan | North | N1 | 壬 | Ren | Yang Water | + | 337.6 - 352.5 |
| | | N2 | 子 | Zi | Rat (Yang Water) | - | 352.6 - 7.5 |
| | | N3 | 癸 | Gui | Yin Water | - | 7.6 - 22.5 |
| 艮 Gen | Northeast | NE1 | 丑 | Chou | Ox (Yin Earth) | - | 22.6 - 37.5 |
| | | NE2 | 艮 | Gen | Northeast (Earth) | + | 37.6 - 52.5 |
| | | NE3 | 寅 | Yin | Tiger (Yang Wood) | + | 52.6 - 67.5 |
| 震 Zhen | East | E1 | 甲 | Jia | Yang Wood | + | 67.6 - 82.5 |
| | | E2 | 卯 | Mao | Rabbit (Yin Wood) | - | 82.6 - 97.5 |
| | | E3 | 乙 | Yi | Yin Wood | - | 97.6 - 112.5 |
| 巽 Xun | Southeast | SE1 | 辰 | Chen | Dragon (Yang Earth) | - | 112.6 - 127.5 |
| | | SE2 | 巽 | Xun | Southeast (Wood) | + | 127.6 -142.5 |
| | | SE3 | 巳 | Si | Snake (Yin Fire) | + | 142.6 - 157.5 |

玄
空
飛
星
風
水

Within each Mountain, the 3 central degrees are known as the Direct Line, and the remaining 6 degrees to the right and left of the central 3 degrees are known as Seaming Right or Seaming Left Lines. In advanced Feng Shui, the 24 Mountains can be further divided into the 60 Dragons, the 72 Dragons and even the 120 Gold Divisions, but this is usually for more complex San He Feng Shui formulas. At this stage, focus on familiarising yourself with the 24 Mountains and the direction they correspond with, so that you are able to move onto the most important part of the practical skills associated with Feng Shui: Taking a direction.

*Mastery Academy students taking directions with their Luo Pans during the Mastery Academy China Excursion.*

玄
空
飛
星
風
水

# The Art of Taking a Direction

Taking a direction is one of the most important basic skills that must be mastered before any Feng Shui-ing can be done. Even the most simple and basic systems of Feng Shui, like Eight Mansions Feng Shui, require a direction. This is because the direction of the property serves as the reference point for all the subsequent computations. In the case of Flying Stars, you need to have the Facing Direction of a property in order to plot a Flying Stars chart. Just as in the study of BaZi, the Day Master is the key reference point for the entire chart, so the direction of a property is its key reference point.

The reason why taking a direction is an art is because it is not always easy to establish the Facing of a property. The Facing of the property is essentially the direction that the property faces. Sounds straightforward, right? How hard is it to tell which way the building faces surely? In practice, it is not always easy to establish which way a building faces. Sometimes it's obvious, sometimes it's not. For example, which way does a round building face?

*Can you tell which direction this building faces?*

玄
空
飛
星
風
水

When it comes to determining the facing, it is important to first be aware of the common mistakes that people often make, when it comes to taking a direction. The first and most common mistake is assuming the facing of a property is always the direction that the Main Door faces. Whilst frequently, the Main Door's direction is the same as that of the Facing, that is not the same as saying the direction the Main Door faces is the Facing Direction. Take a look at the illustrations below:

**A**

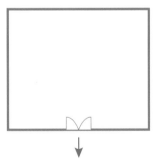

Main Door Facing + House Facing (Facade)

*The door facing and the house facing are the same direction.*

玄
空
飛
星
風
水

B

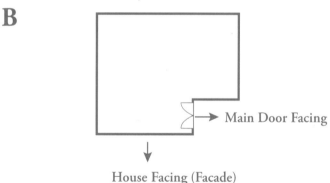

Main Door Facing

House Facing (Facade)

*The door facing and the house facing in this example are not the same direction. In such cases, you always base the facing direction on the direction the house faces, NOT the door.*

In Diagram A, the Main Door and the Facing are the same direction. In Diagram B, the Main Door and the Facing are not the same direction and using the Main Door to determine the Facing will result in an incorrect direction and therefore, an incorrect Flying Stars chart.

玄
空
飛
星
風
水

The Main Door's direction is not always the direction that the building faces. In the old days, the Facing of the building would usually be synonymous with the Facing of the Main Door. This is a typical architectural feature in older buildings and houses in China. As such, one could use the Main Door to determine the facing direction. With modern architecture, this is not always the case. A building can have its Main Doors at the sides or even the back of a building but yet have a Façade that faces another direction.

*As these two pictures illustrate, the Main Door Facing is not always the same as the House Facing.*

玄
空
飛
星
風
水

Thus, in modern times, one cannot assume safely that the Facing of the building, and the Facing of the Main Door, are one and the same. The only exception to this rule is when is it difficult to determine the orientation of the building, perhaps due to the nature of the architectural design, or when there are many roads around the property and it is hard to determine which road it was built to face. In such instances, the Main Door is regarded as indicative of the Facing of the building.

But as a general rule, we DO NOT use the Main Door direction only to determine the Facing of the property. We always determine the Facing of the property independently from the facing of the Main Door. Of course, the Main Door's direction is one of the factors that is taken into consideration when seeking to determine the building's Facing direction, but it is not always the decisive factor, except in specific instances.

So what are the factors that you should consider in determining the Facing of a building? First, you should consider the orientation of the building. Which way does the building look like it is built to face? Some buildings are built to face a park view, an ocean view or an open space.

*This house is built to face the river view*

玄
空
飛
星
風
水

*This house is built to face the road*

Secondly, consider the most Yang side of the building. Yang of course, translates to activity and movement, so look to which is the busiest area around the building (such as a main street, or a busy road) and then look to see if that is also the direction that the building is orientated to face. Yang also can be said to be the part of the building that receives the most light, although again, you must be cautious when considering this factor as some buildings are now designed to enable light to enter the building from all directions.

Only after you have considered all these factors, do we consider the direction of the Main Door. And even then, the Main Door's direction is used in tandem with the factors above, to arrive at a conclusion as to the Facing direction of a building.

玄
空
飛
星
風
水

# How to take a direction using a Luo Pan

Once you have ascertained the Facing, stand in the center of the Facing of the building or structure, with your back to the building or structure, and looking out.

*Stand at the center of the house Facing, looking out to take a direction using a Luo Pan.*

Hold up your Luo Pan or compass and wait for the needle to settle itself and steady. If the needle continues to fluctuate, then it is possible the door frame or the building is emanating a strong electro-magnetic force that is disrupting the ability of the Luo Pan or compass to orientate itself to the magnetic North. The answer? Simple. Stand a little further in front or behind the Facing and take the direction from there. Remember, at all times, you must look outwards.

Once the needle steadies itself, turn the 24 Mountains ring until the round end of the needle is aligned between the two red dots. (this will not be necessary if you are using the automatic compass as it will automatically give you the direction you are facing).

To determine the direction of the facing, look at which sector the red string is aligned over – you will get a sector reading and a degree reading this way. You now have the Facing direction of the property. Once you have this, you can then plot the Flying Stars chart of the property.

玄
空
飛
星
風
水

*Step 1: Hold up the Luo Pan and wait for the needle to stop moving.*

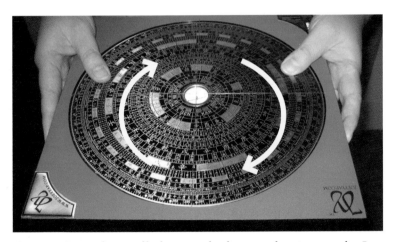

*Step 2: Once the needle has steadied, turn the ring on the Luo Pan using your thumbs.*

玄
空
飛
星
風
水

*Step 3: Align the rounded end of the needle with the two red dots.*

*Step 4: The Facing direction is determined by looking at the direction indicated by the red string.*

玄
空
飛
星
風
水

# Taking a Direction using the Mini Feng Shui Compass

If you are using my automatic Mini Feng Shui Compass, this is slightly easier. First, stand in front of the facing side of the building, with your back to the building and hold up the mini-compass.

玄空飛星風水

The dial will automatically rotate and align itself with the Facing direction of the property.

*Mini Feng Shui Compass.*

玄
空
飛
星
風
水

# Taking a Direction at an Apartment or Non-Landed Property

Apartments, condominiums and non-landed property need to be treated a little bit differently when it comes to taking a direction. Taking a direction at an apartment or condominium (or any kind of high rise building) is often a source of confusion for students and enthusiasts of Feng Shui.

There are many misconceptions people have about taking the direction of an apartment or condominium unit. The most typical one is to assume the facing of the apartment or condominium unit is used to determine the Flying Stars chart. I have also heard of people saying that the direction should be taken standing at the guardhouse of the apartment or condominium units.

*The guardhouse is the wrong place to take the Facing direction of an apartment.*

玄
空
飛
星
風
水

One (incorrect) school of thought argues that each unit in the block has its own Facing Direction, as each unit is treated as a 'house' on its own and thus has its own unique facing. Another incorrect school of thought is that the direction of the unit is determined by its balcony or that only the first 9 floors share a common direction and anything above the 9th floor has an individualised direction.

Obviously if one were to give these approaches some thought, it will become clear why these are misconceptions and mis-directions in so far as ascertaining a Facing Direction of an apartment or condominium is concerned. Each unit cannot have its own Facing Direction, be it based on balcony, door or being above the 9th floor, simply because ultimately, they form part of a larger structure or entity, which is the apartment block. As long as they are under one roof, they share a single Facing and a single Flying Stars chart.

Where the units are clustered together but do not share the roof and have several entrances, then you need to pay a little more attention. But as a general rule, you use the building as a whole, including its Façade, to determine the Facing and never use the unit to determine the Facing. The unit's direction is also relevant but this is used later, when it comes to super-imposing the Natal chart on the property. To obtain the basic Flying Star chart of an apartment, we always use the Facing of the entire apartment block where the unit is located.

玄
空
飛
星
風
水

A possible tricky situation is when the building does not appear to have an obvious Facing. This is a common situation with architecturally sophisticated apartment and condominiums which are designed to give all the residents a good view from all sides, or in luxury developments where the unit takes up an entire floor - in such cases, use the Main Entrance or Main Lobby of that building as the reference point of the Facing. However, this is not applicable in cases where the development has a Master Entrance or Master Lobby which leads to the other buildings.

To take a direction, determine the Facing of your own block or building, using the guidance indicated above. Then, stand at the façade of the building, looking out, and take the direction using the Luo Pan or Mini Feng Shui Compass, following the steps laid out above.

Here are a few examples of how to determine the Facing of apartments.

*Facing*

*Facing*

玄
空
飛
星
風
水

*Facing*

*Facing*

玄
空
飛
星
風
水

# Facing and Sitting Directions

Once you have established the Facing direction, you automatically have what is known as the 'Sitting' of the house. This is the direction that is 180 degrees opposite of the Facing Direction.

Look at the example below. Let's say you've measured the Facing of a property and found that it faces South.

180 degrees opposite of South is North. So the Facing of this property is South, and the Sitting is North.

Normally, we will mark out the Sitting and Facing of a property using special markers. The arrow (↑) marks the Facing, whilst the inverse T (⊥) marks the Sitting. Typically, the floor plan will be marked like the example below:

*Facing Direction*

*Sitting Direction*

Once you have the Facing and Sitting Direction of the property in hand, you are now ready to plot the Qi map of the property, using Xuan Kong Flying Stars.

玄空飛星風水

Chapter 5:

# Flying the Stars

玄空飛星風水

**5**

玄
空
飛
星
風
水

Without the Flying Stars chart of a property, it is not possible to make use of all the information and theories that have been discussed in Chapters 2 and 3. Xuan Kong Flying Stars is mainly about tapping into the right kind of Qi, through the use of the right sectors of a property, and the location of important rooms in the appropriate sectors.

The Flying Stars chart enables us not only to know which are the favourable and unfavourable sectors of a property, but also the precise type of Qi that is affecting those sectors. It is, in essence, a map of the Qi in a property. The 'stars' in Flying Stars, refer to different bodies of Qi.

The ability to understand the nature of the Qi affecting a particular sector is what gives Xuan Kong Flying Stars its 'predictive' or 'divination' aspects. As this is a basic beginner's book, I will not be going into the predictive or divination aspects of Xuan Kong Flying Stars in this book. It will be explored in my subsequent books in the **_Xuan Kong Feng Shui_** series.

In this book, I will focus on showing you how to determine the favourable and unfavourable sectors of a property by plotting the Flying Stars chart of a property. You will also learn how to evaluate the Qi quality of the three important aspects in a property - the main door, kitchen and bedroom – using a Flying Stars chart. You will then be able to see how a lot of the fundamental theories and foundation that you have read in Chapters 2 and 3 come together.

Learning how to fly the stars takes a little bit of practice. It's not difficult but it does require a little effort. For convenience, I have prepared a set of blank 9 box grids at the back of this chapter so just make photocopies and practice using those grids.

玄
空
飛
星
風
水

# Anatomy of a Flying Stars Chart

This is what a basic Flying Stars chart, also known as a Natal chart, looks like:

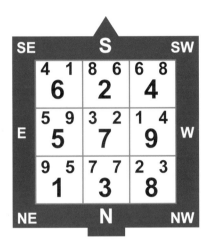

In a Flying Stars chart, there are nine boxes or Palaces. Modern Flying Stars practitioners prefer to reference the Palaces by their directional names, such as the Southwest Palace.

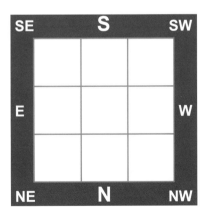

玄
空
飛
星
風
水

Traditionally, Feng Shui practitioners refer to Palaces by their original Later Heaven Ba Gua names – for example, the Southwest Palace would be called the Kun Palace, or the North Palace would be referred to as the Kan Palace.

Next, a little bit more terminology. The Palace that matches the Facing direction of the House is referred to as the Facing Palace, and the Palace that matches the Sitting direction of the house is referred as the Sitting Palace. So if a property has a South Facing direction, the South Palace is called the Facing Palace. The North Palace, which is the Sitting Direction, is called the Sitting Palace. The Palace right in the center is called the Central Palace or Heavenly Heart.

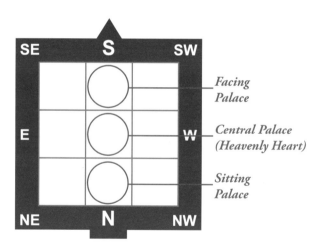

Each of the numbers on a Flying Stars chart represents a star. There are nine types of stars. Each of these nine stars has its own qualities, and in different periods, has a different Qi quality, based on the 5 phases of Qi I talked about in Chapter 3.

On a basic Flying Stars chart, there are always NINE Palaces with nine Base Stars, Sitting Stars and Facing Stars. Each Palace will contain one Base Star, one Sitting Star and one Facing Star. The Base Star is the star in the center of the Palace, the stars on the left and right of the Base Star in each Palace is the Sitting and Facing Star respectively. If you see a diagram that does not conform to this, then it is NOT a Natal Flying Stars chart.

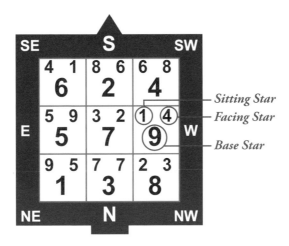

There are other Flying Stars charts that we may eventually use in tandem with the Natal chart, such as the Annual, Monthly or even Daily Star Charts. As this is a beginner's book, I shall focus on the Natal chart as this is the most practical type of chart for most beginners.

When learning how to fly the stars, you will need to first learn how to fly the Base Stars, which is the sequence of numbers that occupy the center of every box. After that, you will learn how to fly the Sitting Stars and Facing Stars. The stars fly in a fixed formation or sequence of movements, based on the central number. So once you have mastered that sequence, flying the stars is nowhere near as hard as learning how to fly!

玄
空
飛
星
風
水

# Return of the Luo Shu

The first step in learning how to fly the stars is to be familiar with what is known as the Luo Shu trail. This is, in essence, the sequence or order of movements in which the stars will fly in a Flying Stars chart – it is the pattern of movement of Qi. This pattern of movement is fixed and we do not deviate from this path of flying the stars, ever. It is the same pattern for ANY star chart, whether it is a Natal star chart, an annual star chart, or a yearly star chart.

The diagram below shows you sequence or path of movement of stars, called the Luo Shu trail.

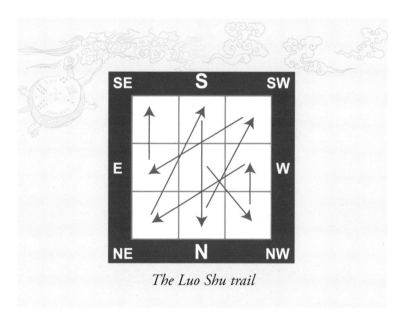

*The Luo Shu trail*

At this point, I have not asked you to incorporate the numbers yet because it is important that you are familiar with the movement sequence involved, before you move on to the numbers.

Use the 9 Grid box at the back of this chapter and practice a couple of times the Luo Shu trail to familiarise yourself with the pattern or sequence of movement. Remember, this trail does not ever change. It is a fixed path. The movement of the stars is always from the center, to the lower right hand box, to the center right hand box and so on.

If you flip back to the diagram of the Luo Shu, you will remember it also contains directional references. The Luo Shu trail actually follows a fixed directional movement – it always moves from the center, to the Northwest, then West, Northeast, South, North, Southwest, East, and finally Southeast.

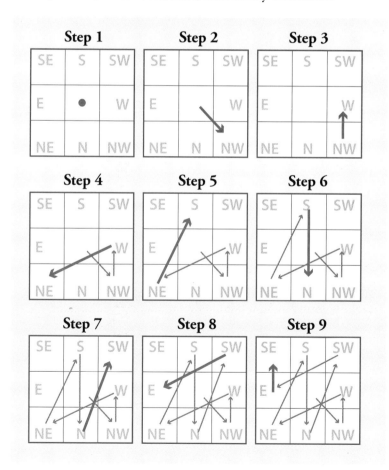

玄
空
飛
星
風
水

# Flying Yin and Flying Yang

Those of you who memorised the Luo Shu's numbers will see that the Luo Shu trail follows a numerical sequence, from the number in the center box. There are in fact TWO numerical sequences that the Luo Shu trail can follow: a Yin sequence and a Yang sequence. We call this Flying the Stars using the Yin Path, and Flying the Stars using the Yang Path.

In a Yang Path, the numbers in the Luo Shu trail go in ascending order, based on the number in the center of the 9 box grid. In a Yin Path, the numbers in the Luo Shu trail proceed in descending order, based on the number in the center of the 9 box grid. As there are only 9 boxes, whenever you get to 1, the next number in the sequence is 9. Similarly, when you get to 9, the next number in the sequence is not 10, but 1.

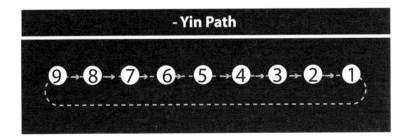

玄
空
飛
星
風
水

# Following the Central Palace

Up to this point, you would be familiar with the Luo Shu trail, which tells you how the stars move, and the Yin and Yang paths, which tells you how the numbers are sequenced – either in a forward sequence, or reverse sequence, based on the number in the Central Palace.

Clearly, in order to fly the stars, you will need to have the Central Palace number. How do you ascertain what is the number in the Central Palace? The center number is always determined by what is termed the 'Period Luck' of the property.

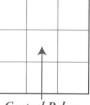

*Central Palace*

The Period Luck of the property is determined by the move-in date. The move-in date is the point in time that the residents of the property occupy or live at the property. We then correspond that date with the Period Luck Table to determine the Period Luck of the property.

| Cycle 元 | Period 運 | Year 年 | Gua 卦 |
|---|---|---|---|
| **上** Upper | 1 | 1864 - 1883 | ☵ 坎 Kan |
| | 2 | 1884 - 1903 | ☷ 坤 Kun |
| | 3 | 1904 - 1923 | ☳ 震 Zhen |
| **中** Middle | 4 | 1924 - 1943 | ☴ 巽 Xun |
| | 5 | 1944 - 1963 | - |
| | 6 | 1964 - 1983 | ☰ 乾 Qian |
| **下** Lower | 7 | 1984 - 2003 | ☱ 兑 Dui |
| | 8 | 2004 - 2023 | ☶ 艮 Gen |
| | 9 | 2024 - 2043 | ☲ 離 Li |

玄
空
飛
星
風
水

So for example, if a person moves into their property in 2006, their property's Period Luck is 8, as they moved into the property during Period 8 (2004-2023). Similarly, if the person moved into their property in 1982, then the property's Period Luck is 6, as they moved into the property during Period 6 (1964-1983).

There are some Feng Shui practitioners who argue that it is the date that the property was built that is the reference point. I do not agree with this standpoint because this does not conform with an important fundamental principle in Feng Shui, which is the Cosmic Trinity. A property can only be said to be occupied when people (the Man component) move into the property. If the property is newly-built but not occupied, then the Man aspect of Heaven-Earth-Man is not fulfilled.

玄
空
飛
星
風
水

Thus, if a property was built in 1987, but only first occupied in 2004, then it is a Period 8 building. If the property was built in 1980 and the owners moved into the property in 1985, then it is a Period 7 building. However, if a property is built in 1980, and the first owner moved in in 1983, then it is a Period 6 building. Note that I said first owner. If the subsequent owner moved in only a week after the first owner moved out, this property is still considered Period 6.

With apartments, the Period Luck of the building is dictated by the first person who moved into the building. Accordingly, although the unit is vacant, as long as the building has been occupied, then the Period Luck of the building starts at the point it was first occupied, and not at the point the particular unit became occupied. Thus, if an apartment was built in 1980, and the first occupant moved into their apartment in 1985, the building is a Period 7 building and remains a Period 7 building, irrespective of the occupants moving in and out.

Once you have ascertained the Period Luck of a building, you have what we call the Base Number for the chart.

玄
空
飛
星
風
水

# The Base Chart 運盤

The Base Number is also known as the Period Plate 運盤 (Yun Pan) in Flying Stars and is determined by the Period Luck of the house. With the Base Number, you can now fly the Base Stars to determine what we call the Base Chart of the property.

How do you fly the Base Stars? Based on the Base Number, you fly the stars in a Yang path, or in an ascending numerical sequence.

Let's take an example to show you how it's done. Let's say the property is a Period 7 property. Place 7 in the Central Palace.

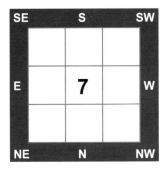

Now, fly the stars in a Yang path, or a ascending numerical sequence, meaning, from 7, go to 8, then 9, then 1 and so on, following the Luo Shu trail. The Base Star Chart will look like this:

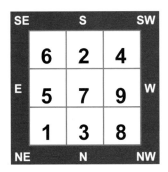

玄
空
飛
星
風
水

If the property is a Period 8 property, then we simply change the Base Number, and then fly the stars, again in the Yang path or forward numerical sequence, following the Luo Shu trail.

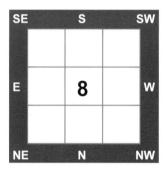

The Base Star Chart for a Period 8 property will look like this:

| SE | S | SW |
|---|---|---|
| 7 | 3 | 5 |
| 6 | 8 | 1 |
| 2 | 4 | 9 |
| NE | N | NW |

Okay, now that you have the Base Star Chart of the property in hand, it's time to move on to the Sitting and Facing Stars. The process of ascertaining the Sitting and Facing Stars is again very similar to how we derived the Base Star Chart. It's simply a matter of knowing where to start.

玄
空
飛
星
風
水

# The Sitting Stars 坐星

Sitting Stars are sometimes referred to as Mountain Stars. But the correct terminology in Xuan Kong Flying Stars is Sitting Star 坐星 (Zuo Xing). Mountain Stars is a term used in advanced Xuan Kong to refer to actual Mountain Formations and is not synonymous with Sitting Stars although at beginner level, the terms appear interchangeable. However, at this level, it is better to simply regard them as Sitting Stars.

Sitting Stars are the stars on the left hand side of the Base Star in every Palace. It is said in the ancient classics that "Mountain governs People, Water governs Wealth" 山管人丁,水管財 (Shan Guan Ren Ding, Shui Guan Cai). As such, Sitting Stars relate to health and relationship aspects and are referenced whenever we are interested in understanding the impact of a property's Qi on the health and relationship issues of the residents of a property.

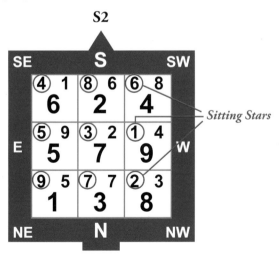

To plot the Sitting Stars, we need a reference Star, in the same way we needed the Base Star in the central palace, to plot the Base Star chart. The Sitting Star reference Star is based on the Base Star that occupies the Sitting Palace of the Flying Stars chart.

玄
空
飛
星
風
水

To determine the reference Star for the Sitting Stars, we place the Base Number of the Sitting Palace, in the top left hand corner of the Central Palace. This is now the first Sitting Star, and the kick-off point for us to plot our Sitting Stars.

Let's take an example to show you how to fly the Sitting Stars.

This property is a Period 8 property with a South 2 午 (Wu) Facing Direction. We know South is the Facing Palace, therefore the Sitting Palace will be North. In the North palace, there is the Base Star #4. So, we place #4 in the Sitting Star position, in the Central Palace.

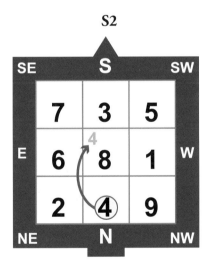

Now, from here, you simply follow the Luo Shu trail and fly the stars. But before you do that, you have to determine if the Sitting Stars will fly Yin or Yang Path, based on the Facing direction of the building or property.

玄
空
飛
星
風
水

| Sector Number | Sector 1 | Sector 2 | Sector 3 |
|---|---|---|---|
| **1, 3, 7, 9** | + (Yang) | - (Yin) | - (Yin) |
| **2, 4, 6, 8** | - (Yin) | + (Yang) | + (Yang) |
| **5 (Odd)** | + (Yang) | - (Yin) | - (Yin) |
| **5 (Even)** | - (Yin) | + (Yang) | + (Yang) |

*Star Path Table*

The Star Path table above tells you when the Sitting and Facing Stars will fly Yin and when they will fly Yang. The sub-sector refers to the directional sub-sector of the property's Facing (i.e. SW1, NW2, E3) and the odd/even number refers to the Sitting or Facing Star's number.

So in our example above, the property faces S2. That means the sub-sector is sub-sector 2. The star we want to fly is the #4 star, which is an even number. Referencing the Star Path table, the star flies in the Yang path, which is in an ascending numerical sequence. So from 4, it goes to 5, and so on and so forth, following the Luo Shu trail.

Now, let's plot the Sitting Stars for this South 2 午 (Wu) property.

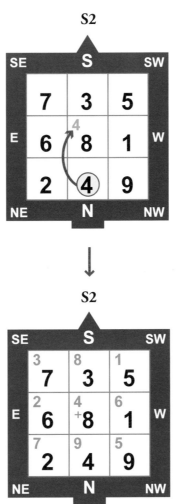

See, we're already half way there! Now, on to the Facing Stars.

玄
空
飛
星
風
水

# Facing Stars 向星

Facing Stars are also sometimes referred to as Water Stars. I prefer however at the beginner level, to use the correct term Facing Star 向星 (Xiang Xing). Water Stars in advanced Xuan Kong, actually refer to physical Water formations. Facing Stars govern matters related to Wealth and Career. Thus, whenever we are interested in understanding the impact of the stars on Wealth-related matters in a property, we look at the Facing Stars. The Facing Stars are located on the right hand side of the Base Star in every Palace.

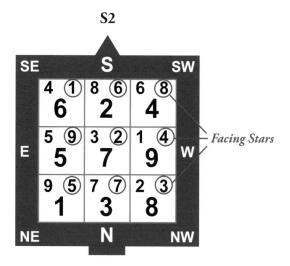

The Facing Stars are plotted based on the Base Star in the Facing Palace of a property. The method used to plot the Sitting Stars is the same as the method used to plot the Facing Stars. It is simply the reference Star that changes. With the Sitting Star, the Sitting Palace Base Number is used. With the Facing Star, the Facing Palace Base Number is used.

Similarly, the sequence that the stars fly (Yin or Yang Path) is determined by the same Star Path table used to determine the path of the Sitting Stars.

玄
空
飛
星
風
水

Let's now take a look at our previous example of a Period 8 property with a South 2 午 (Wu) Facing Direction. In a South 2 午 (Wu) Facing property, the Base Star #3 is located in the Facing Palace. So, place the #3 star as the Facing Star in the Central Palace.

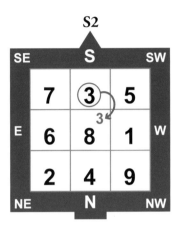

S2

|  SE | S | SW |
|---|---|---|
| 7 | ③ | 5 |
| 6 | 8 | 1 |
| 2 | 4 | 9 |
| NE | N | NW |

#3 is an odd number and South 2 午 (Wu) is in sub-sector 2 – so according to our Star Path table, that means the stars will fly a Yin path.

| Sector Number \ Sector | Sector 1 | Sector 2 | Sector 3 |
|---|---|---|---|
| 1, 3, 7, 9 | + (Yang) | - (Yin) | - (Yin) |
| 2, 4, 6, 8 | - (Yin) | + (Yang) | + (Yang) |
| 5 (Odd) | + (Yang) | - (Yin) | - (Yin) |
| 5 (Even) | - (Yin) | + (Yang) | + (Yang) |

玄空飛星風水

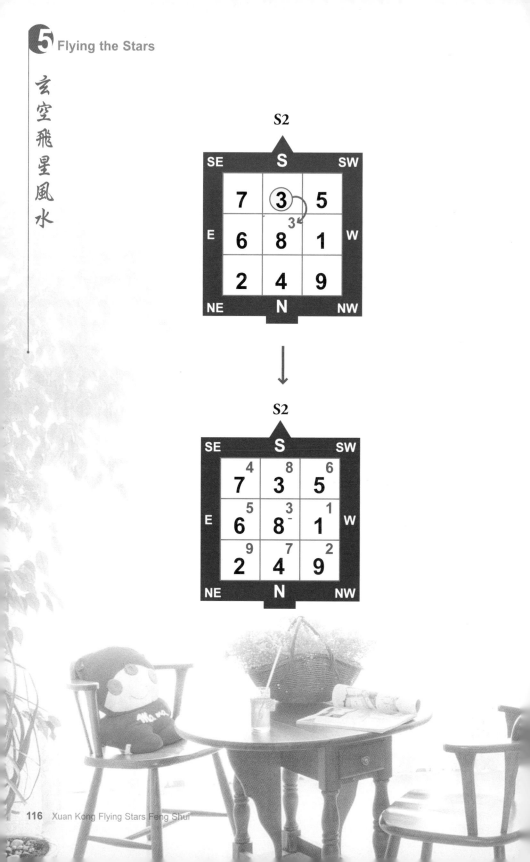

玄空飛星風水

Now, when you put it all together, this is what a complete Flying Stars chart for a property Facing S2, in Period 8, looks like this:

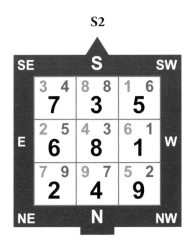

S2

| SE | S | SW |
|---|---|---|
| 3 4<br>**7** | 8 8<br>**3** | 1 6<br>**5** |
| E  2 5<br>**6** | 4 3<br>**8** | 6 1<br>**1**  W |
| 7 9<br>**2** | 9 7<br>**4** | 5 2<br>**9** |
| NE | N | NW |

■ **Facing Stars** ■ **Sitting Stars** ■ **Base Stars**
向星 坐星 運星

玄
空
飛
星
風
水

Let's do another example. Let's take the example of a Period 7 property, facing Southwest 3 申 (Shen). As the governing Period is Period 7, we place 7 as the Base Star in the Central Palace.

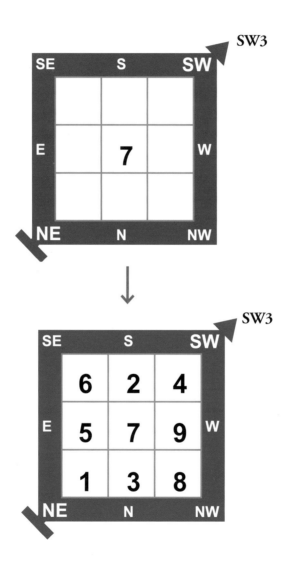

玄
空
飛
星
風
水

Now, let's fly the Sitting Stars. The House faces Southwest 3 申 (Shen), so the Sitting of the house, which is always opposite the Facing, is Northeast 3 寅 (Yin) . Look at the Northeast Palace – the Base Star in that Palace is the #1. Place the #1 in the top LEFT corner of the Central Palace. We now have the reference number to fly our Sitting Stars.

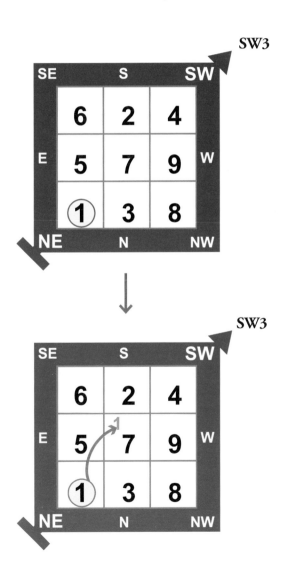

玄
空
飛
星
風
水

| Sector Number | Sector 1 | Sector 2 | Sector 3 |
|---|---|---|---|
| 1, 3, 7, 9 | + (Yang) | - (Yin) | - (Yin) |
| 2, 4, 6, 8 | - (Yin) | + (Yang) | + (Yang) |
| 5 (Odd) | + (Yang) | - (Yin) | - (Yin) |
| 5 (Even) | - (Yin) | + (Yang) | + (Yang) |

Now we need to determine if the Sitting Stars will fly Yin or Yang. Now, #1 is an odd number. So when we look at the Star Path table, we know that an odd number, which is in the sub-sector 3, should fly the Yin path. So the Sitting Stars fly in a descending numerical sequence. The Sitting Stars for a Period 7, SW3 申 (Shen) Facing property are as follows:

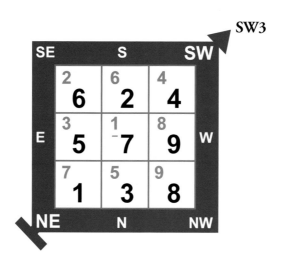

玄
空
飛
星
風
水

What about the Facing Stars? This time, we look at the Facing Palace or the Southwest Palace. The Base Star in the Facing Palace is #4.

Transfer the #4 star to the Facing Star position in the Central Palace. Now, we need to determine the path the #4 star will fly. Again, we look at the Star Path table. The #4 star is an even number and when in the third sub-sector, it flies the Yang path. So the Facing Stars will fly in an ascending numerical sequence.

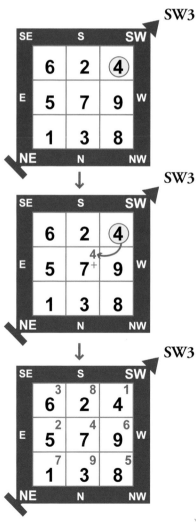

玄空飛星風水

The complete Flying Star chart for a Period 7, Southwest 3 Facing property looks like this:

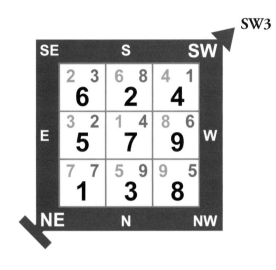

SW3

| SE | S | SW |
|---|---|---|
| 2 3 **6** | 6 8 **2** | 4 1 **4** |
| 3 2 **5** (E) | 1 4 **7** | 8 6 **9** (W) |
| 7 7 **1** (NE) | 5 9 **3** (N) | 9 5 **8** (NW) |

■ **Facing Stars**
向星

■ **Sitting Stars**
坐星

■ **Base Stars**
運星

## Yin and Yang of the #5

You will notice that there is a special provision in the Star Path table for the #5 star. In the original Luo Shu, the #5 resides in the center. It has no direction assigned to it. If you look at the Luck Cycle reference table, Period 5 has no Trigram or Gua associated with it.

| | | | | |
|---|---|---|---|---|
| SE | | S | | SW |
| | 4 | 9 | 2 | |
| E | 3 | 5 | 7 | W |
| | 8 | 1 | 6 | |
| NE | | N | | NW |

Therefore, we can say that #5 is like a floating or dynamic star and so has its own set of rules on when it flies Yin and when it flies Yang.

This set of rules is only applicable whenever the #5 resides in either the Sitting or Facing Palace as the Base Number. As the Sitting and Facing Stars are based on the Base Number of the Sitting and Facing Palace, the special rule relating to the #5 is only applicable when #5 actually resides in these Palaces as the Base Number.

| | | | | |
|---|---|---|---|---|
| SE | | S | | SW |
| | 6 | 2 | 4 | |
| E | (5) | 7 | 9 | W ▶ W1 |
| | 1 | 3 | 8 | |
| NE | | N | | NW |

*#5 in Sitting Palace*

| | | | | |
|---|---|---|---|---|
| SE | | S | | SW ↗ SW1 |
| | 7 | 3 | (5) | |
| E | 6 | 8 | 1 | W |
| | 2 | 4 | 9 | |
| NE | | N | | NW |

*#5 in Facing Palace*

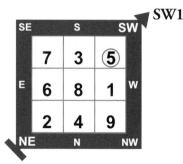

玄
空
飛
星
風
水

Which way the #5 flies is dependant on the Base Star in the Central Palace. The rule goes like this: if the Central Palace Base Star, which is also the Period Luck, is an odd number (1,3,7,9) then the stars fly in as if they are odd numbers. If the Central Palace Base Star is an even number (2,4,6,8) then the stars fly in accordance with the even number sequence.

| Sector Number | Sector 1 | Sector 2 | Sector 3 |
|---|---|---|---|
| **1, 3, 7, 9** | + (Yang) | - (Yin) | - (Yin) |
| **2, 4, 6, 8** | - (Yin) | + (Yang) | + (Yang) |
| **5 (Odd)** | + (Yang) | - (Yin) | - (Yin) |
| **5 (Even)** | - (Yin) | + (Yang) | + (Yang) |

玄
空
飛
星
風
水

Let's take an example to show you how it works. In Period 7, in a West 1 Facing property, #5 is the Base Star for the East Palace. Assuming the East Palace is also your Sitting Palace, your Sitting Stars will be flown, using the #5 as the first star or reference star.

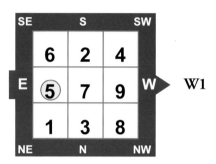

In Period 7, the Base Star in the Central Palace is 7. 7 is an odd number. Therefore, we follow the rule applicable to odd 5. West 1 is sub-sector 1, so the stars will fly in a Yang path.

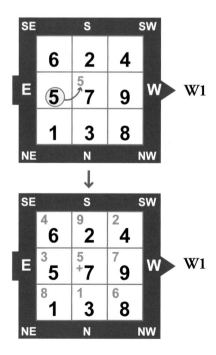

玄空飛星風水

Let's change things a little bit and change the Facing of the property. Now you have a Period 7, West 2 Facing property, and #5 is the Base Star for the East Palace, which is also the Sitting Palace.

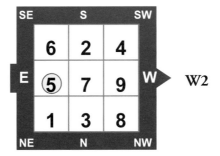

We still use the odd number star sequence because the Base Star number is the same, which is 7. But instead of flying the stars Yang, the stars will now fly Yin as the sub-sector has changed.

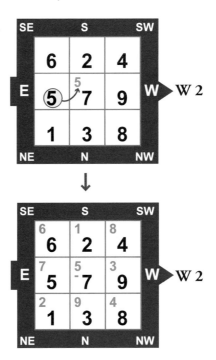

Let's try an example where the #5 is in the Facing Palace. In this Period 8, Southwest 1 Facing property, #5 is the Base Star in the Facing Palace.

**SW1**

|  |  |  |
|:---:|:---:|:---:|
| SE | S | SW |
| 7 | 3 | ⑤ |
| E  6 | 8 | 1  W |
| 2 | 4 | 9 |
| NE | N | NW |

Now we have to determine which way the Facing Stars will fly, using the #5. First, we check the Base Number in the Central Palace. 8 is an even number. Second, we look at the sub-sector reference. This is a Southwest 1 Facing property, so sub-sector 1 is the relevant sub-sector. According to our Star Path table, the stars should fly Yin, meaning in a descending numerical order.

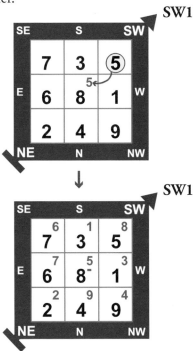

玄
空
飛
星
風
水

Again, let's adjust the example slightly. We now have a Period 8, Southwest 2 Facing property, with #5 as the Base Star in the Facing Palace.

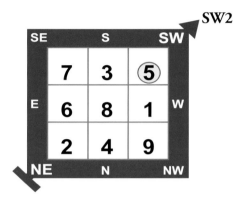

The Base Number of the Central Palace has not changed, so we only need to reference the different sub-sector. Southwest 2 is sub-sector 2, so the stars will fly Yang, or in an ascending numerical order.

| Sector Number | Sector 1 | Sector 2 | Sector 3 |
|---|---|---|---|
| **1, 3, 7, 9** | + (Yang) | - (Yin) | - (Yin) |
| **2, 4, 6, 8** | - (Yin) | + (Yang) | + (Yang) |
| **5 (Odd)** | + (Yang) | - (Yin) | - (Yin) |
| **5 (Even)** | - (Yin) | + (Yang) | + (Yang) |

玄空飛星風水

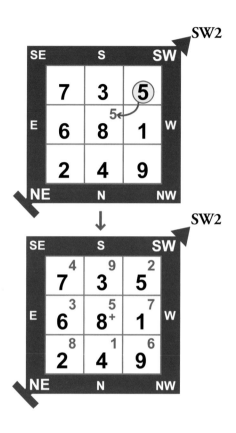

With the #5, it is simply a matter of knowing what the Base Number in the Central Palace (which is also the Period Luck of the property), and then referencing the correct sub-sector based on the Facing direction of the property. The stars are still flown the same way, using the Luo Shu trail, either Yin or Yang.

## Super-imposing the Natal chart onto a Property

Once you have the property's Natal chart, you still need to super-impose this onto the property's floor plans proper. This is something which most beginners usually find challenging so I will show you how it is done, step-by-step.

In order to super-impose the property's Natal chart onto the property's floor plans, you need a copy of the floor plans. Preferably, use an architect's version of the floor plans as this will be more accurate. Then, you need the basic Natal Flying Stars chart of the property with you as well.

Let's say the property is a North 2, Period 8 Facing property. So, the Natal chart for the property is as below:

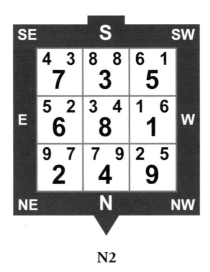

N2

玄
空
飛
星
風
水

Now, draw a 9 box Grid over the floor plan of the property.

Now, mark out the 9 Palaces, using the Facing Palace as a reference. We know this property faces North. So mark North in the Facing Palace, and mark the other directional palaces out accordingly.

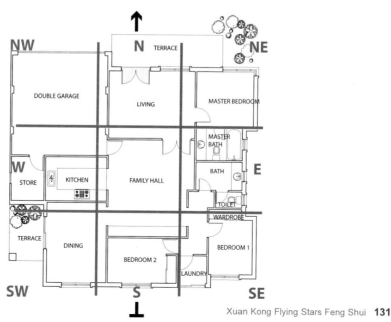

玄
空
飛
星
風
水

To super-impose the Natal chart into the property, we just transfer the respective Flying Stars (Base, Sitting and Facing Stars) into the relevant palaces. So the Flying Stars in the North Palace of the Natal chart, we transfer into the North Palace of the property's floor chart, and so on for each of the Palaces.

**Step 1: Transfer the stars in the North Palace, to the North Palace of the property.**

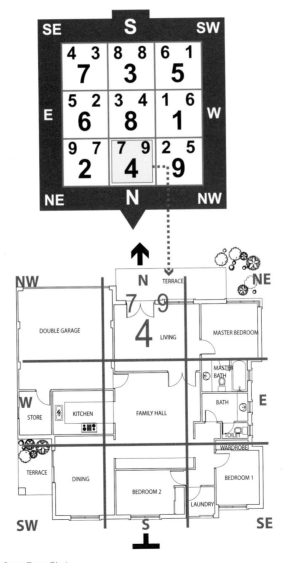

## Step 2: Transfer the stars in the Northeast Palace, to the Northeast Palace of the property.

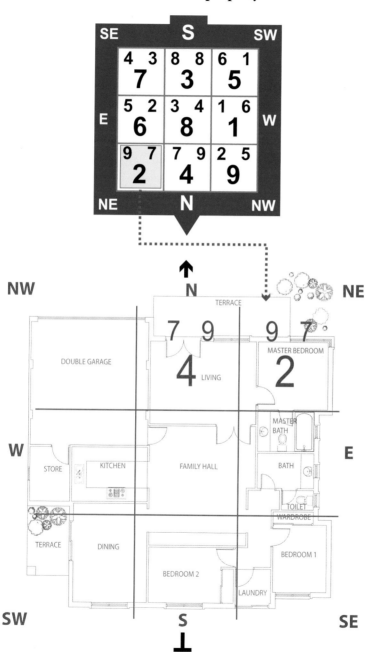

玄空飛星風水

**Step 3: Transfer the stars in the East Palace, to the East Palace of the property.**

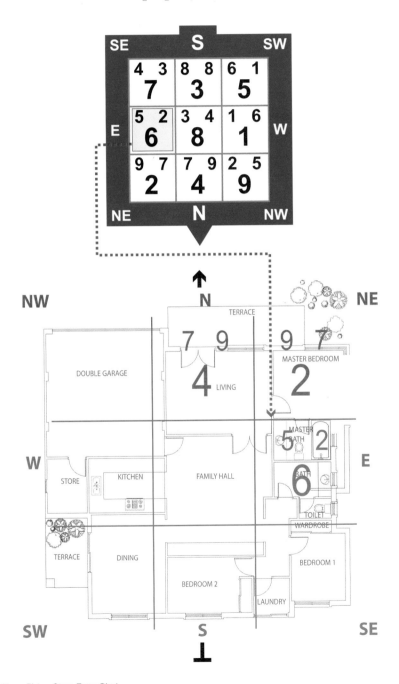

玄空飛星風水

**Step 4 : Transfer the stars in the Southeast Palace, to the Southeast Palace of the property.**

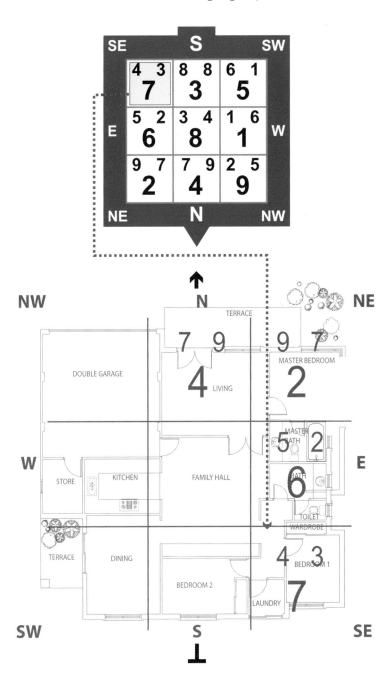

玄空飛星風水

**Step 5:** Transfer the stars in the South Palace, to the South
Palace of the property.

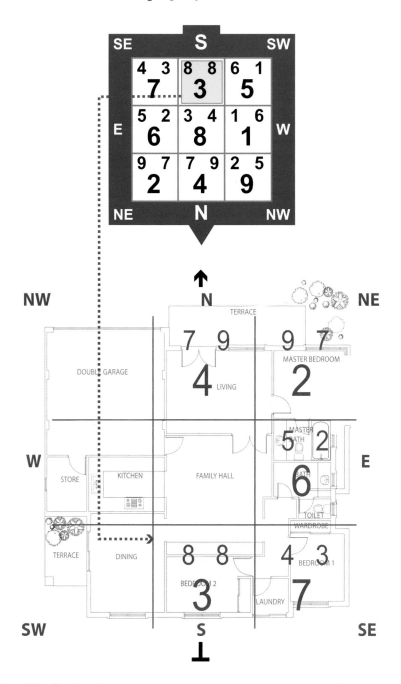

玄空飛星風水

## Step 6 : Transfer the stars in the Southwest Palace, to the Southwest Palace of the property.

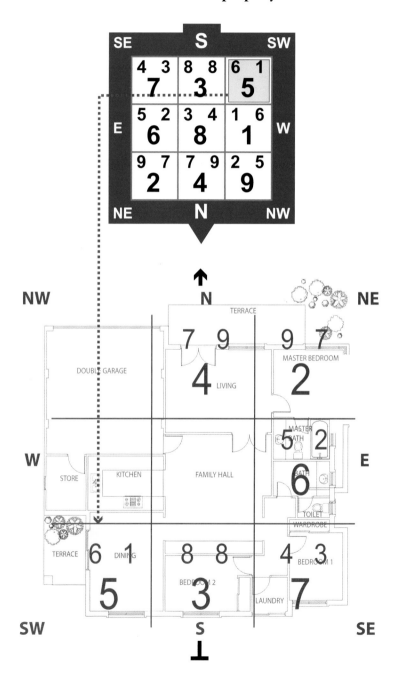

玄
空
飛
星
風
水

**Step 7: Transfer the stars in the West Palace, to the West Palace of the property.**

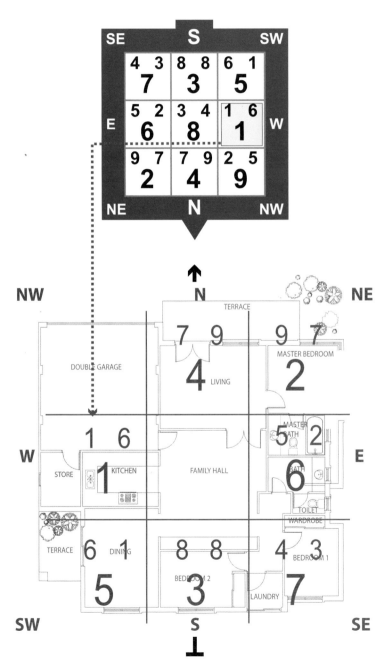

玄空飛星風水

**Step 8: Transfer the stars in the Northwest Palace, to the Northwest Palace of the property.**

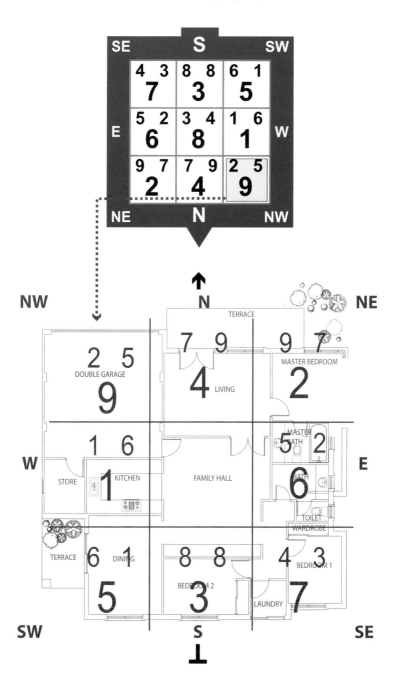

玄空飛星風水

**Step 9: Transfer the stars in the Central Palace, to the Central Palace of the property.**

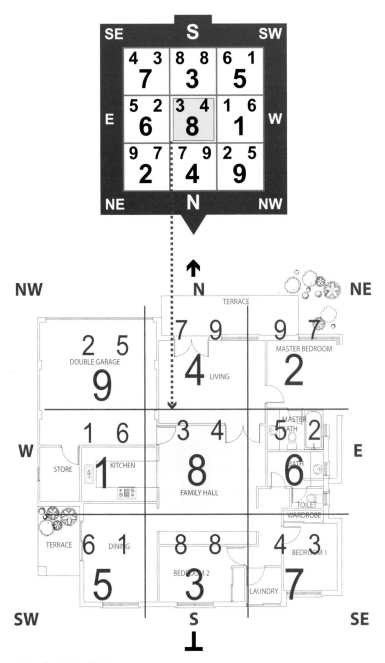

玄
空
飛
星
風
水

With the Flying Stars transferred onto the property's floor plans, using the 9 Grids, you can now see which Flying Stars are in which part of your property, specifically which rooms contain which Flying Stars, and which Combinations.

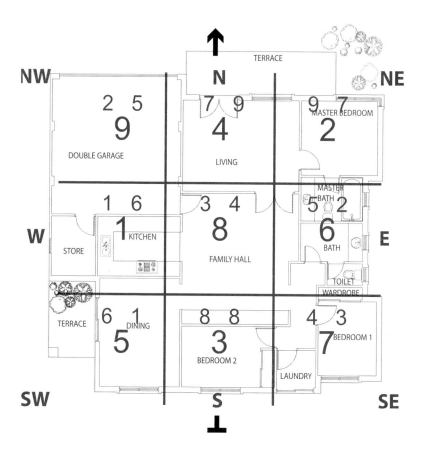

玄
空
飛
星
風
水

The process involves one extra step when it comes to an apartment or condominium, that is orientating yourself on the North/South directions of your unit. This is because for apartments, we need to first determine the Flying Stars chart based on the entire apartment building's facing. Then, we super-impose the Flying Stars chart that we have plotted (based on the Building's facing) over our unit.

All you have to do is get the directional orientation of your unit. Then transfer the stars to the respective palaces accordingly.

Let's take a look at an example. This is the floor plan of an apartment. The apartment building faces West 2. The unit we are looking at has its balcony in the East.

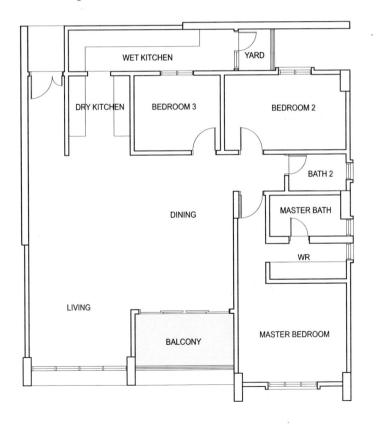

玄
空
飛
星
風
水

Divide up the apartment using the 9 Grids system and mark out the directions.

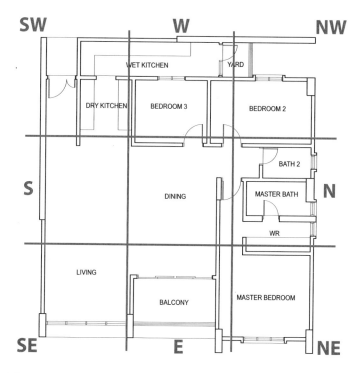

The apartment block faces W2 and it is a Period 7 building. This is the Flying Stars chart of the apartment block.

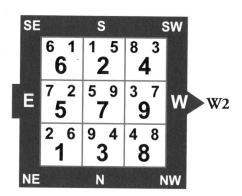

玄空飛星風水

Transfer the stars from the W2, Period 7 Flying Stars chart, onto the 9 grids of the apartment unit, palace by palace.

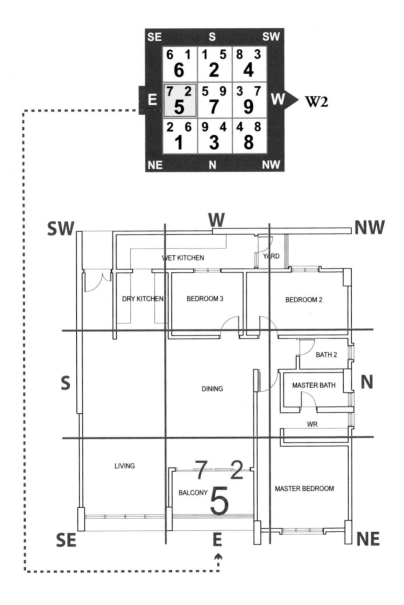

玄空飛星風水

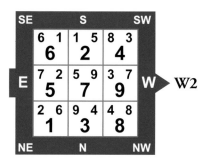

*Transfer the stars into the respective palaces*

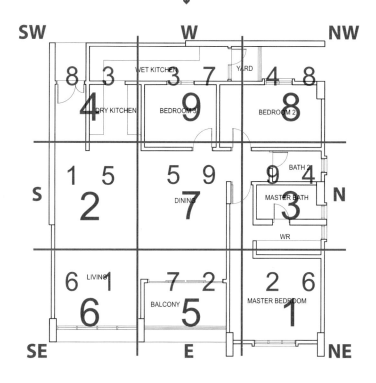

玄
空
飛
星
風
水

## Fly Fly Fly!

Now, ideally, I would recommend you plot all 16 charts for all the 1-9 Periods for practice. This will enable you to really master how to fly the stars and be extremely familiar with the Luo Shu trail. However, for relevance, you really probably only need to be familiar with the Flying Stars charts for Periods 7 and 8 at this point in time. Those of you who prefer the more high-tech approach, you can use the Flying Stars calculator on my website: ***www.joeyyap.com***

However, those who intend to master Xuan Kong Flying Stars should consider plotting all the charts manually for Periods 6, 7 and 8. For reference (and so you can check the answers after you've practiced manual plotting), I have included at the end of this chapter, a complete set of all the Flying Star charts for all the directions, in every period.

玄
空
飛
星
風
水

# Forms and Flying Stars

Although Xuan Kong is part of the San Yuan school of Feng Shui and thus, places greater emphasis on the aspect of time, this does not mean Forms or Luan Tou, are ignored. A key principle in Flying Stars Feng Shui states: "*Forms activate the stars, star in turn affect the residents*". As you advance in your understanding of Xuan Kong Flying Stars Feng Shui, you will learn that Flying Stars cannot be considered in isolation and that it is important to pay attention to the external Forms and how they affect the stars in the chart. This is why the Sitting Stars are sometimes called Mountain Stars because they are affected by external and internal Mountain Forms. Similarly, that is why Facing Stars are called Water Stars because they are affected by external and internal Water Forms.

Chapter 7 and 8 will delve a little into the use of Forms and provide you with a basic understanding of Forms and Flying Stars. My subsequent books on Flying Stars will also expand the discussion on Forms and how they impact the Flying Stars of a property. For now focus on the fundamentals and learning the basics like plotting the charts and super-imposing them onto a property. In the next chapter, I'll show you how to do some basic, simple interpretation of a Flying Stars chart, beginning with the meaning of each of the Nine Stars.

玄空飛星風水

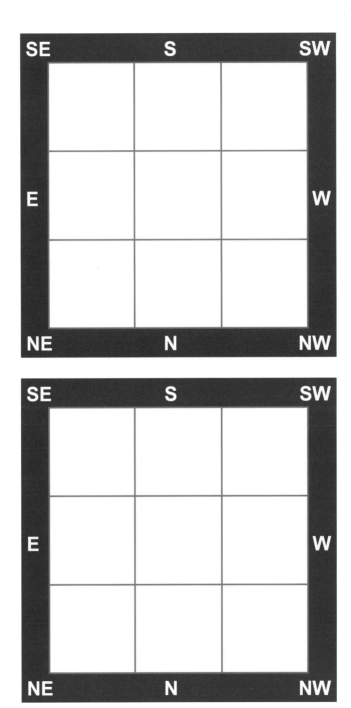

玄
空
飛
星
風
水

# Flying Stars Charts
# Period 1 - 9

玄空飛星風水

## Period 1 一運

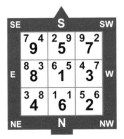

Sitting N1
Facing S1

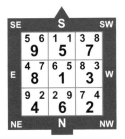

Sitting N2/N3
Facing S2/S3

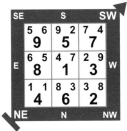

Sitting NE1
Facing SW1

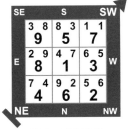

Sitting NE2/NE3
Facing SW2/SW3

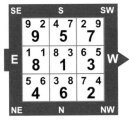

Sitting E1
Facing W1

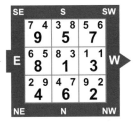

Sitting E2/E3
Facing W2/W3

Sitting SE1
Facing NW1

Sitting SE2/SE3
Facing NW2/NW3

玄空飛星風水

# Period 1 一運

Sitting S1
Facing N1

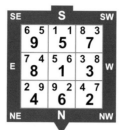

Sitting S2/S3
Facing N2/N3

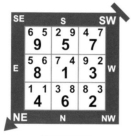

Sitting SW1
Facing NE1

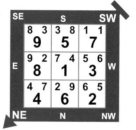

Sitting SW2/SW3
Facing NE2/NE3

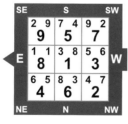

Sitting W1
Facing E1

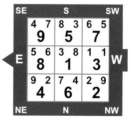

Sitting W2/W3
Facing E2/E3

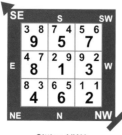

Sitting NW1
Facing SE1

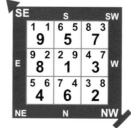

Sitting NW2/NW3
Facing SE2/SE3

玄空飛星風水

## Period 2 二運

Sitting N1
Facing S1

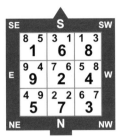

Sitting N2/N3
Facing S2/S3

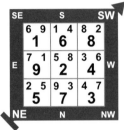

Sitting NE1
Facing SW1

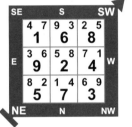

Sitting NE2/NE3
Facing SW2/SW3

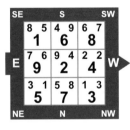

Sitting E1
Facing W1

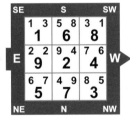

Sitting E2/E3
Facing W2/W3

Sitting SE1
Facing NW1

Sitting SE2/SE3
Facing NW2/NW3

# Period 2 二運

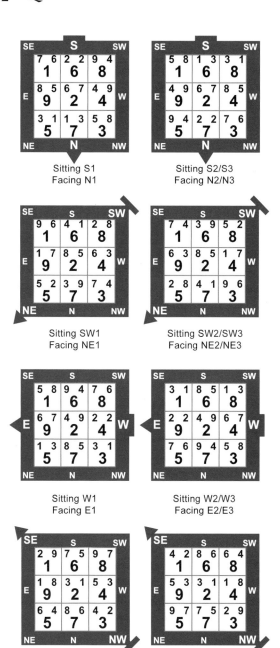

Sitting S1
Facing N1

Sitting S2/S3
Facing N2/N3

Sitting SW1
Facing NE1

Sitting SW2/SW3
Facing NE2/NE3

Sitting W1
Facing E1

Sitting W2/W3
Facing E2/E3

Sitting NW1
Facing SE1

Sitting NW2/NW3
Facing SE2/SE3

玄空飛星風水

## Period 3 三運

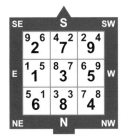

Sitting N1
Facing S1

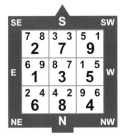

Sitting N2/N3
Facing S2/S3

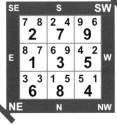

Sitting NE1
Facing SW1

Sitting NE2/NE3
Facing SW2/SW3

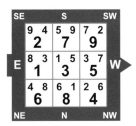

Sitting E1
Facing W1

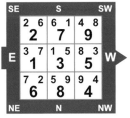

Sitting E2/E3
Facing W2/W3

Sitting SE1
Facing NW1

Sitting SE2/SE3
Facing NW2/NW3

# Period 3 三運

玄空飛星風水

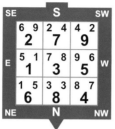

Sitting S1
Facing N1

Sitting S2/S3
Facing N2/N3

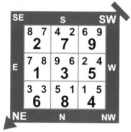

Sitting SW1
Facing NE1

Sitting SW2/SW3
Facing NE2/NE3

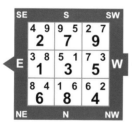

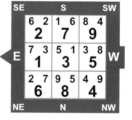

Sitting W1
Facing E1

Sitting W2/W3
Facing E2/E3

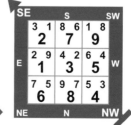

Sitting NW1
Facing SE1

Sitting NW2/NW3
Facing SE2/SE3

玄空飛星風水

## Period 4 四運

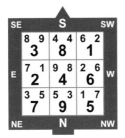

Sitting N1
Facing S1

Sitting N2/N3
Facing S2/S3

Sitting NE1
Facing SW1

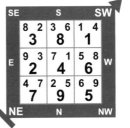

Sitting NE2/NE3
Facing SW2/SW3

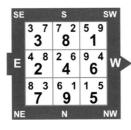

Sitting E1
Facing W1

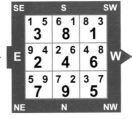

Sitting E2/E3
Facing W2/W3

Sitting SE1
Facing NW1

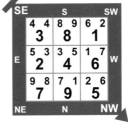

Sitting SE2/SE3
Facing NW2/NW3

玄空飛星風水

## Period 4 四運

Sitting S1
Facing N1

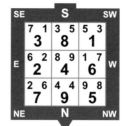

Sitting S2/S3
Facing N2/N3

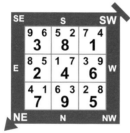

Sitting SW1
Facing NE1

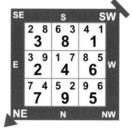

Sitting SW2/SW3
Facing NE2/NE3

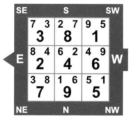

Sitting W1
Facing E1

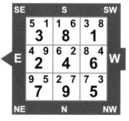

Sitting W2/W3
Facing E2/E3

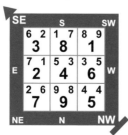

Sitting NW1
Facing SE1

Sitting NW2/NW3
Facing SE2/SE3

玄空飛星風水

## Period 5 五運

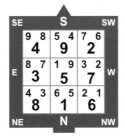

Sitting N1
Facing S1

Sitting N2/N3
Facing S2/S3

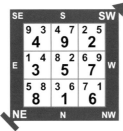

Sitting NE1
Facing SW1

Sitting NE2/NE3
Facing SW2/SW3

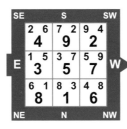

Sitting E1
Facing W1

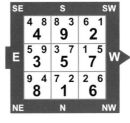

Sitting E2/E3
Facing W2/W3

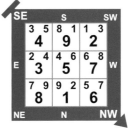

Sitting SE1
Facing NW1

Sitting SE2/SE3
Facing NW2/NW3

玄空飛星風水

# Period 5 五運

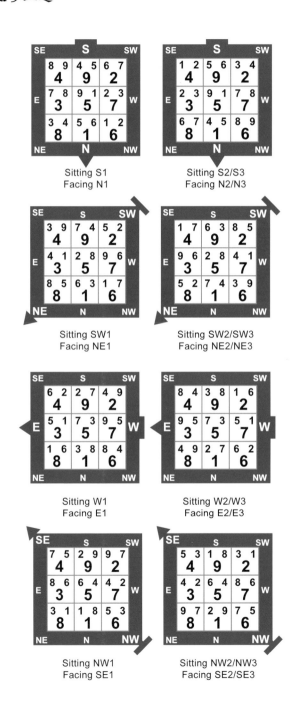

Sitting S1
Facing N1

Sitting S2/S3
Facing N2/N3

Sitting SW1
Facing NE1

Sitting SW2/SW3
Facing NE2/NE3

Sitting W1
Facing E1

Sitting W2/W3
Facing E2/E3

Sitting NW1
Facing SE1

Sitting NW2/NW3
Facing SE2/SE3

玄空飛星風水

## Period 6 六運

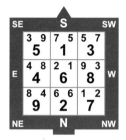

Sitting N1
Facing S1

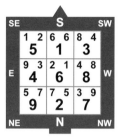

Sitting N2/N3
Facing S2/S3

Sitting NE1
Facing SW1

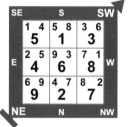

Sitting NE2/NE3
Facing SW2/SW3

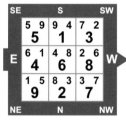

Sitting E1
Facing W1

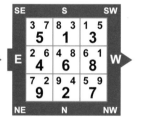

Sitting E2/E3
Facing W2/W3

Sitting SE1
Facing NW1

Sitting SE2/SE3
Facing NW2/NW3

# Period 6 六運

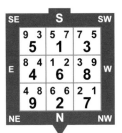

Sitting S1
Facing N1

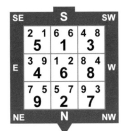

Sitting S2/S3
Facing N2/N3

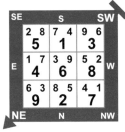

Sitting SW1
Facing NE1

Sitting SW2/SW3
Facing NE2/NE3

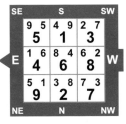

Sitting W1
Facing E1

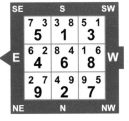

Sitting W2/W3
Facing E2/E3

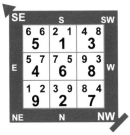

Sitting NW1
Facing SE1

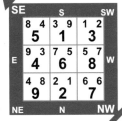

Sitting NW2/NW3
Facing SE2/SE3

玄空飛星風水

## Period 7 七運

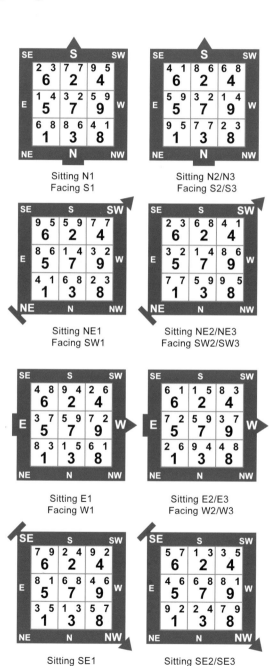

Sitting N1
Facing S1

Sitting N2/N3
Facing S2/S3

Sitting NE1
Facing SW1

Sitting NE2/NE3
Facing SW2/SW3

Sitting E1
Facing W1

Sitting E2/E3
Facing W2/W3

Sitting SE1
Facing NW1

Sitting SE2/SE3
Facing NW2/NW3

玄空飛星風水

## Period 7 七運

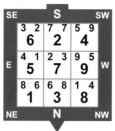

Sitting S1
Facing N1

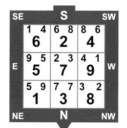

Sitting S2/S3
Facing N2/N3

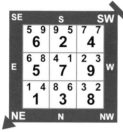

Sitting SW1
Facing NE1

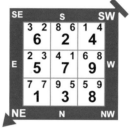

Sitting SW2/SW3
Facing NE2/NE3

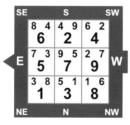

Sitting W1
Facing E1

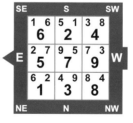

Sitting W2/W3
Facing E2/E3

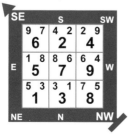

Sitting NW1
Facing SE1

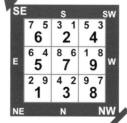

Sitting NW2/NW3
Facing SE2/SE3

玄空飛星風水

### Period 8 八運

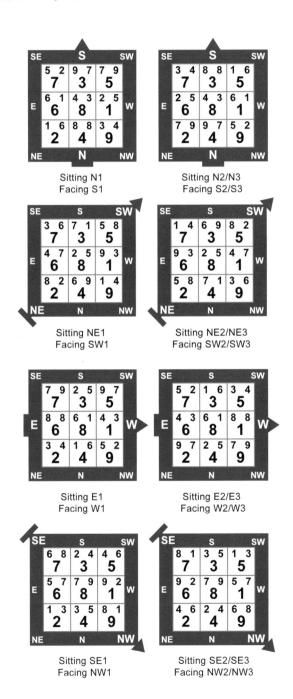

Sitting N1
Facing S1

Sitting N2/N3
Facing S2/S3

Sitting NE1
Facing SW1

Sitting NE2/NE3
Facing SW2/SW3

Sitting E1
Facing W1

Sitting E2/E3
Facing W2/W3

Sitting SE1
Facing NW1

Sitting SE2/SE3
Facing NW2/NW3

玄空飛星風水

## Period 8 八運

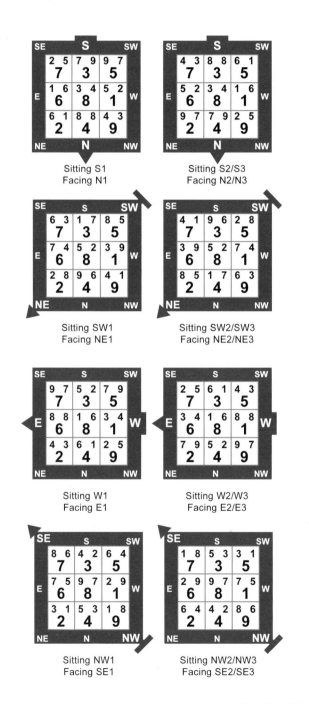

Sitting S1
Facing N1

Sitting S2/S3
Facing N2/N3

Sitting SW1
Facing NE1

Sitting SW2/SW3
Facing NE2/NE3

Sitting W1
Facing E1

Sitting W2/W3
Facing E2/E3

Sitting NW1
Facing SE1

Sitting NW2/NW3
Facing SE2/SE3

玄空飛星風水

### Period 9 九運

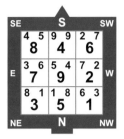

Sitting N1
Facing S1

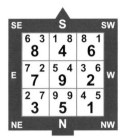

Sitting N2/N3
Facing S2/S3

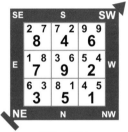

Sitting NE1
Facing SW1

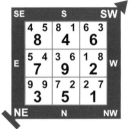

Sitting NE2/NE3
Facing SW2/SW3

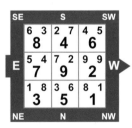

Sitting E1
Facing W1

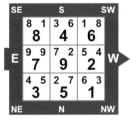

Sitting E2/E3
Facing W2/W3

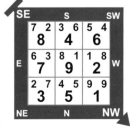

Sitting SE1
Facing NW1

Sitting SE2/SE3
Facing NW2/NW3

玄空飛星風水

# Period 9 九運

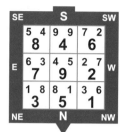

Sitting S1
Facing N1

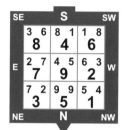

Sitting S2/S3
Facing N2/N3

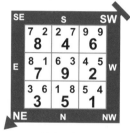

Sitting SW1
Facing NE1

Sitting SW2/SW3
Facing NE2/NE3

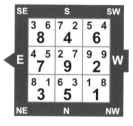

Sitting W1
Facing E1

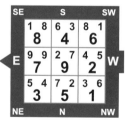

Sitting W2/W3
Facing E2/E3

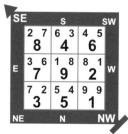

Sitting NW1
Facing SE1

Sitting NW2/NW3
Facing SE2/SE3

Chapter 6:

# Understanding the Nine Stars

玄
空
飛
星
風
水

**B**y this point, you have learnt how to plot the Qi map or energy map of a property, using Flying Stars. You have also learnt how to determine which stars are residing in which part of your property, through the super-imposing of the Flying Stars chart onto the property's house plan, using the 9 Grids. But at this point, all it is to you is a bunch of numbers in boxes, on a floor plan of your property, right? So, it is now time for you to gain a greater understanding of what the nine stars represent. By understanding the attributes and qualities of each of the nine stars, then you will be able to interpret the Qi map of the property, and understand what the numbers are trying to tell you.

When thinking about the nine stars and their attributes, it is very important to recall a few of the fundamental principles I discussed in Chapter 2, particularly the principle of Yin and Yang and the factor of time. The stars have both negative and positive attributes, but which facets will show when you see a particular star, depends on the timeliness and the period. A few of the nine stars are inherently negative, a few are inherently positive in nature and some can be both good and bad. But, even then, we must remember that the stars have the capacity to manifest their positive or negative facets because in Feng Shui, nothing is ever inherently bad or good forever.

玄空飛星風水

The basic principle to remember at this stage of your study is this: when stars are timely, they exert their positive qualities. When stars are untimely, they exert their negative qualities. Of course, this basic principle has exceptions. But at the beginner's stage, I prefer to stick to the big picture, and keep things simple and easy.

Each of the nine stars has an over-riding attribute or quality, but can also be associated with a Trigram or a Gua 卦, an element, a person or relationship, a situation or a part of the human body. However, at this point, I want to show you the attributes of each of the nine stars first. We'll talk about the interpretation of the stars in the next chapter.

玄空飛星風水

# #1 White (一白)

坎 *Kan* ☵ The #1 Star is the star of nobility. This star is also sometimes called the Greedy Wolf Star 貪狼星 (Tan Lang Xing). It is linked with good name, good reputation and status. The #1 Star belongs to the element of Water. Water, in the study of the Five Elements, represents intelligence and wisdom. Hence, the #1 Star also represents emotions, feelings, thinking and thoughts. In terms of businesses, as the element of the #1 Star is Water, thus, it also represents Water-related businesses such as traveling, transportation, logistics, tourism, journalism, fisheries, aquatic businesses, ports and spas, to name a few.

With regard to people, #1 Star represents the middle-aged man, or the middle son of a family. In the Trigrams, the #1 Star is represented by Kan Gua 坎卦.

When the #1 Star is negative or untimely, it brings danger and darkness to the people living (or working) in the area it resides. At its untimely stage, the #1 Star can result in emotional disturbance, emotional instability, psychological problems, danger or obstacles when traveling at sea. Depression is a common problem whenever the #1 Star is untimely or negatively affected by external formations. Other health problems that are commonly brought about by the #1 Star include insomnia, kidney problems, food poisoning, diarrhea or blood-related problems. As the #1 Star represents good name and solid reputation when it is timely, in its untimely or negative stage, the reverse occurs - it brings about problems that result in a bad reputation or tarnished public image.

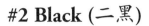

玄空飛星風水

# #2 Black (二黑)

坤
*Kun*
☷

The #2 Black Star is associated with the element of Earth, and Kun Gua 坤卦. The element of Earth, in the study of the Five Elements, is said to be the producer of ten thousand things. It is governed by the Huge Door Star 巨門星 (Ju Men Xing). Thus, the #2 Star relates to success with regard to property, assets, real estate, capital gains and residual income or passive income from land-related transactions.

Kun Gua relates to the mother figure, thus the #2 Star can also represent the mother figure or the eldest woman in the property. But it also can represent a motherly figure, such as a nanny or a caretaker.

In terms of the body, the #2 Star represents the stomach and digestive systems. Thus, whenever the #2 Star is affected by negative external forms, such as a pylon or a sharp roof, stomach problems are likely. In minor cases, it means persistent

玄
空
飛
星
風
水

digestive problems but in serious cases, it can indicate stomach cancer. Objects-wise, the #2 Star represents a cow, or items that come in twos.

When the #2 Star is untimely and manifesting its negative qualities, it often brings about illness. The #2 Star is often regarded as the Illness Star 病符星 (Bing Fu Xing) in basic Flying Stars Feng Shui. Generally, where #2 Star resides, the resident occupying that room is prone to falling sick frequently.

Specifically, the #2 indicates illness affecting elderly ladies, or even miscarriages (when the #2 Star meets the #1 Star, in combination or in an annual or monthly star). When the #2 Star is not timely, problems include property-related disasters, natural disasters such as landslides or earthquakes, and property-related investment problems or loss of wealth from bad property investments.

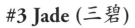

# #3 Jade (三碧)

震
*Zhen*

The #3 Jade Star is the star of changes, perseverance, aggressive drive and determination, movement and forward momentum. It is governed by the Rewards Star 祿存星 (Lu Cun Xing). The #3 Star is an active vibrant star and thus is usually favourable for those who are professional sportsmen or who have jobs that involve a lot of movement and aggression such as police personnel, sports coaches, military personnel and SWAT personnel.

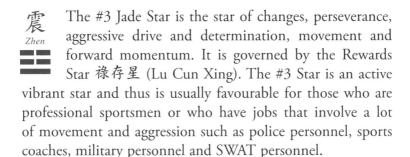

The #3 Star is associated with Zhen Gua 震卦, or the Thunder trigram. Thus, just like thunder, it relates to kicking things off, starting something new, embarking on a new project and changing directions or goals.

玄
空
飛
星
風
水

For people matters, the #3 Star represents the eldest son of the family. With regard to parts of the body, the #3 Star relates to the legs or feet. Thus, where the #3 Star is negatively affected by say a T-junction, the resident using the room with the #3 Star may experience injuries to the feet or legs.

Typically, using the #3 Star represents engaging in high-risk businesses endeavours or businesses that involve danger or adventure as the #3 Star is a daring and gung-ho star. For example, theme parks or bungee jumping or sport-related businesses would represent adventurous and dangerous businesses. When timely, the #3 Star represents taking calculated risks in business or financial matters, as well as success achieved from hands-on efforts. Those of you who are familiar with BaZi, the #3 Star is similar to the controlled 7 Killings star.

When negative or untimely, the #3 Star brings aggression or conflict-based problems such as gossip, rumour-mongering, disputes, back-stabbing, and lawsuits. It is the star of misunderstandings and problems caused by losing one's cool or temper too quickly. When there is a problem with the #3 Star, usually there is also a loss of money caused by legal problems or disputes. When untimely, the #3 Star causes health problems related to the liver or limbs.

玄空飛星風水

# #4 Green (四綠)

巽
*Xun*

The #4 Green Star is the scholar star, governed by the Literary Arts Star 文曲星 (Wen Qu Xing) . It is a star of learning, beauty, achievement through scholarly or literary pursuits, a star of academia and studying. This is why when it is timely, the #4 Star is usually used in the study room or for children who need to study or pass an exam. The #4 Star can also be used by authors, academics, and can represent financial success from books, screenplays, music or creative and artistic endeavours. The #4 Star is similar to the Eating God star in BaZi. It is the star of knowledge, of appreciating fine art and the finer things in life, and is a star that is associated with learning new skills.

玄
空
飛
星
風
水

The #4 Star is associated with Xun Gua 巽卦. With the appropriate use of Water formations, the #4 Star can also manifest Peach Blossom qualities. It brings about romance and positive relationships, with regard to both work and personal life. Thus, the #4 Star is also favourable for businesses that involve relationship-building such as sales, marketing and public-relations.

The #4 Star has a slightly fickle nature – when timely it indicates quick thinking, quick reflexes and an adaptive mind and nature towards endeavours. In terms of the body, the #4 Star represents the hip and the buttocks. Objects-wise, it represents flowers, leaves and grass.

When the #4 Star is untimely, it brings about scandals, adultery, and fickleness. This is because #4 is associated with Xun Gua, which is the Wind. The wind is always changing direction and is rarely stable or constant. Thus, it represents the wandering person, brings about aimlessness and the inability to focus on academic or scholarly pursuits. It is also possible that immoral behaviour or relationship problems will manifest if the #4 Star is affected by unfavourable water formations as the #4 Star is linked to Peach Blossom.

# #5 Yellow (五黃)

Leader

Generally, the #5 Yellow is a negative star. This is because it is not associated with any Trigram and thus is governed by the Chastity Star 廉貞星 (Lian Zhen Xing). In Feng Shui, the Chastity Star is a volatile, aggressive and menacing star and thus is usually seen as having negative characteristics and attributes.

As this is a beginner's text, you should assume #5 has a mainly negative quality. At the advance level, there are exceptions to the rule on the negative nature of #5 Yellow Star, and its menacing and aggressive characteristics can be 'tamed' and turned positive, manifesting in ultimate wealth, great power, and tremendous status and nobility. This is because the Chastity Star is also sometimes called the Emperor-producing star, governing high power leadership and great authority. However, at the beginner level, you should play things safe and err on the side of caution by treating the #5 as a negative star.

The #5 Yellow Star typically brings negative outcomes of a catastrophic level. Fatal accidents, bankruptcy, significant illness, betrayal in the family or in business and never-ending problems are some of the problems the #5 Yellow brings. The #5 tends to exert its malignant effects on the stars around it as well, so handling the #5 is very important.

Now, out of 9 Palaces on your Natal chart, two palaces will contain the #5 Star either as a Sitting or Facing Star and one palace will contain the #5 Star as the Base Star. Do not be alarmed – remember, all Flying Stars need to be triggered or activated in order for any of their negative or positive qualities to manifest. As long as the #5 Star is not triggered or activated, or there are positive external forms, the #5 Star is not a problem.

玄
空
飛
星
風
水

# # 6 White (六白)

乾
*Qian*

The #6 White Star is the star of authority, power and status. The #6 Star represents status, power and authority that is bestowed, that is attained and comes from climbing up the corporate ladder or tenure in public service. The #6 Star is associated with the Military Arts Star 武曲星 (Wu Qu Xing), and Qian Gua 乾卦. Unlike the #1 Star, which relates to status and nobility that is already existent or given (for example, the person is already titled or an important person), the #6 Star relates to position that is obtained, often through hard work and perseverance. Hence, later, as you delve into star combinations, you will learn that a #6 and #1 stars together, indicates tremendous power and authority that is both bestowed and obtained, such as becoming the CEO of the company or Prime Minister or President of a country. It indicates being able to wield authority and yet have scholarly wisdom.

In terms of the body, the #6 White Star represents the head and the brain. This star also represents the father, the eldest male in a family, the leader or Managing Director/CEO in a company. When the #6 White's negative qualities are triggered, problems associated with authority are likely. Health-wise, a negative #6 White results in the residents of the property experiencing frequent migraines, headaches or in serious cases, injuries to the head.

Qian Gua is associated with extreme Yang so when it is negative or untimely, the #6 Star brings loneliness and great solitude. When very negative, it also brings about a loss of power, a sudden downfall, great change (from employment to retirement for example) and sometimes, results in individuals leaving the family home, occupants of the property experiencing violent death or violence-related harmful incidents.

玄
空
飛
星
風
水

# # 7 Red (七赤)

兑
*Dui*

The #7 Red Star is generally not a positive star although it has some positive attributes, notably, speaking and communication skills and financial or business success or wealth achieved from speaking or communicating.

The #7 Star is represented by Dui Gua 兑卦 and also associated with the Broken Soldier Star 破軍星 (Po Jun Xing). Dui Gua represents the mouth, hence the #7 Star is associated with actors and performers, as well as people with jobs that involve talking, speaking or communicating. In the family, this star represents the youngest daughter in the family. It also represents surgeons and dentists, as the #7 Star is akin to a small knife.

#7 has aspects of Peach Blossom or romance qualities. Thus when the #7 is negative or untimely, it can also represent problems caused by Peach Blossom such as sexual disease. Of course, it can also represent an ulcer in the mouth in minor cases, since #7 is associated with the mouth.

When untimely and exerting its negative attributes, the #7 Star indicates health problems that require operations or surgery. Dui Gua after all represents the small knife, thus the association with operations and surgical procedures. Negative external forms that cause the #7 Star to exert its negative aspects also increased mean risk of robbery, being held hostage or blackmailed, or accidents that involve cuts or nicks, or being bitten. In extreme instances, it can indicate being murdered.

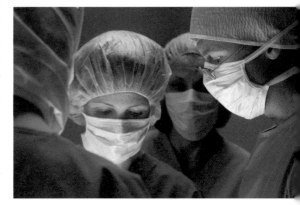

玄空飛星風水

# # 8 White (八白)

艮
*Gen*

☶

The #8 Star's primary attribute is prosperity and wealth. It is usually regarded as a positive star. It does have some negative attributes, which manifest when the star is untimely, but these are quite minimal and frequently not a cause for great concern. The #8 Star is one of the few stars that has a more positive nature and tends to exert its positive sides. At the beginner's stage, it is safe to assume that the #8 White Star is generally a good star and mainly governs financial aspects.

This star indicates wealth obtained as a result of hard work and personal efforts. It represents wealth obtained through legitimate old-fashioned hard work and perseverance. The #8 Star is represented by the Left Assistant Star 左輔弼 (Zuo Fu Bi), and Gen Gua 艮卦. In terms of the body, the #8 Star represents the back, the spine, the nose and extremities like the fingers. In terms of people, the #8 Star represents the youngest male child of the family.

When timely, the #8 Star indicates financial boom. When untimely, its negative effects are greater on young children under the age of 12 (because #8 represents the youngest child). As #8 is the wealth star, when it is untimely, it indicates problems related to money such as thriftiness, being calculative and tight-fistedness. Health-wise, #8 when negative indicates lingering or long-term illness that is niggling but usually not fatal.

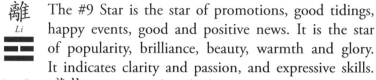

玄空飛星風水

# #9 Purple (九紫)

離
*Li*

The #9 Star is the star of promotions, good tidings, happy events, good and positive news. It is the star of popularity, brilliance, beauty, warmth and glory. It indicates clarity and passion, and expressive skills. Li Gua 離卦 is associated with the #9 Star. The #9 Star is also known as the Right Assistant Star 輔弼星 (Fu Bi Xing). Those who are familiar with BaZi, the #9 star is similar to the Hurting Officer star. The star usually causes individuals to be demonstrative, to seek to show their talents to the world, and to seek to draw attention to their abilities.

In terms of people, the #9 Star represents the middle daughter or a middle-aged woman. In terms of the body, this Star represents the eyes and the heart.

When manifesting its negative attributes, the #9 Star brings about sadness, a feeling of being down in the dumps and depression. Career-wise, the #9 Star, when untimely, indicates demotion or a decline in one's career resulting in a feeling of discontent, a backward step as it were. Problems are often the result of inability to express oneself or communication issues, such as misunderstandings caused by what the person says. Health problems associated with an untimely #9 Star include eye problems and heart problems.

Now that we've covered the attributes of all the nine stars, we are ready to use this understanding in the context of the Flying Stars of a property. In the next chapter, I will show you how to engage in some simple interpretations of the Flying Stars in a property, using the attributes of the nine stars we have discussed in this chapter.

玄
空
飛
星
風
水

**I**n the previous chapter, you learnt how to fly the stars and how to super-impose the Natal chart onto the floor plan of your property. Now, plotting the Flying Stars chart and learning how to super-impose it onto a floor plan is a technical skill. With any Natal chart, the interpretation is always of greater significance and importance than the technical ability to plot the chart. What is the point in knowing what stars are in what location in your property if you have no idea what it means or how to use it, right?

So in this chapter, we are going to focus on the most important aspect of Flying Stars, which is the interpretation and practical usage, something that many Flying Stars books usually don't tell you about.

First, we need to be able to place some context to the terms 'interpretation' and 'practical usage'. Interpretation means understanding the Qi map of the property, as determined from the Flying Stars in the various sectors. We are trying to find the prosperous or favourable areas or rooms of the property, and at the same time, identify the unfavourable areas or rooms in the property. We aslo want to determine which stars are relevant to which aspect of the residents' lives and needs.

玄
空
飛
星
風
水

To do this, we must understand which stars govern what matters, as well as be able to ascertain which stars are timely, and which stars are untimely, based on the Time factor. Remember what I said in Chapter 6 about how when stars are timely they exert their positive features during certain Periods and when they are untimely they exert their negative features during certain Periods?

I will focus on the interpretation of the Natal chart from two aspects: the nature of the star itself, which I have discussed in Chapter 6 and the type of star (Sitting Star or Facing Star). As you advance in your understanding and study of Xuan Kong Flying Stars, we will add in other types of stars into the equation (the Base Star, the Monthly and Annual Stars, in tandem with the Facing and Sitting Stars), the Star Combinations, the Residents and even Xuan Kong Date Selection.

What about practical usage? That refers to understanding how to make use of the favourable and unfavourable areas or rooms in the property. To do this, we must understand how to power up the stars. We need to know what activates and de-activates a star. Facing and Sitting Stars are activated and de-activated in different ways. I will show you how Forms can activate or de-activate a star – however at this point, because this is a beginner's book, I will not discuss Forms in great depth and I will keep the discussion to simple basic common forms. I will talk about more sophisticated and larger Forms in my subsequent books in this *Xuan Kong Flying Stars* series.

玄
空
飛
星
風
水

## Money or People Matters?

But before we delve into interpretation proper, we must first have a greater understanding of the Facing and Sitting Stars, specifically, in terms of what issues they govern.

It is said in the classics Mountain governs People, Water governs Wealth 山管人丁，水管財 (Shan Guan Ren Ding, Shui Guan Cai). This simple but very important mantra affords us a key principle in interpreting and applying Flying Stars.

In essence, what this mantra is telling us is that every time there is an issue or matter that relates to wealth, career, money, income or a person's livelihood, the Facing Star is the star that we focus on. Meaning – we should read the Facing Star. If health state, family matters (such as children or fertility), personal or work relationships are the issue or matter in question, then the Sitting Star is what we focus on in the Natal chart.

This of course is a simplified outlook towards Wealth versus People Matters. At an advanced level of Flying Stars, one has to actually scrutinise the matter or issue and determine if it is really a cut-and-dried money or people matter and whether it is an external issue (involving outsiders) or an internal issue (involving family members).

In my experience, it is RARE for a situation to be purely about money or health/family alone. If you have a health problem, money is needed to solve the problem surely. Similarly, if your job involves relationships (such as private banking, or public relations), your wealth or income is directly determined to a degree by your ability to build relationships.

玄空飛星風水

In the early days of Flying Stars practice, the Facing Star was frequently given more emphasis or attention, compared to the Sitting Star. However, today, wealth, career and matters related to money are frequently inter-linked with health, relationships and family matters. Also, society has evolved. People are interested not just in either money or family, but 'work-life balance'. So, in fact, both the Facing and the Sitting Stars must be considered and utilised.

In advanced Feng Shui, we also have to consider the speed in which outcomes are achieved. Sitting Stars usually take longer to show results, as they are Yin in nature. Facing Stars by contrast usually show quicker results – anywhere within 2 weeks to a month to bring about a change in the outcomes. So if the problem is a health problem, but we want the problem to be resolved quickly, a Flying Stars practitioner may use a Facing Star, even though the Sitting Star governs the Health issues.

At this beginner's stage, a clear-cut perspective is acceptable. But as you advance in your understanding of Xuan Kong Feng Shui, you need to think in a more sophisticated manner and not regard the problems faced by the residents simplistically. For now however, just remember that with regard to wealth issues and money matters, we look at Facing Stars. For health and family as well as relationship matters, we look at the Sitting Stars.

玄
空
飛
星
風
水

## Powering up the Stars

Now that you understand which star (Facing or Sitting) to look at with regard to money matters and people matters, you must understand how the stars are activated and de-activated.

Understanding how to apply Flying Stars is like learning how to use the lights in your house. Knowing which aspect (money or people) is controlled by which star (Sitting or Facing Stars) is like knowing which switch in your house turns on which light. Understanding how to activate or de-activate the stars is therefore understanding how to turn on the lights or flip the switch to turn on the lights. In order for a star's qualities or attributes to manifest, the star must be activated.

Now, in the previous chapter, I mentioned the need to consider the factor of Forms or Luan Tou of your property. When it comes to Flying Stars, it is important to remember this key principle: *Forms activate the Stars, and the Stars in turn influence the People.* So when we want to understand if a star has been activated or 'switched on' or not, we must

therefore look at the external Forms, or what is immediately outside the property, to see if the star in that sector is being activated.

So, what type of Forms activate which type of star? Let's start with the Facing Star.

玄空飛星風水

The Facing Star as you have already learnt in the previous chapter is the active star. It is a star with Yang attributes. Accordingly, it is activated by or receptive to Yang features in the environment.

What are Yang features? The most obvious example of a Yang feature is real water, in the form of a lake or pond or pool. Roads, doorways, corridors, gates, junctions and lower ground can also be considered Yang features. This is the reason why Facing Stars are also sometimes called Water Stars in some books.

玄
空
飛
星
風
水

So what activates or switches on the Sitting Star? Sitting Stars have a Yin nature and thus are activated by Yin features in the environment. What is a Yin feature? The most obvious example of a Yin feature is a mountain or a hill. Higher ground, or a large building or solid structure can also be considered Yin features. Trees are usually not considered Yin features. This is the reason why Sitting Stars are also sometimes called Mountain Stars.

Now, you know how to turn on the lights, but you also need to know how to turn them off, right? So, in addition to understanding how Sitting and Facing Stars are activated, we must also know how they are de-activated.

Again, it's pretty simple and a case of the opposites. Facing Stars are activated by Yang features (water, junctions, lower ground) and accordingly, Yin features will de-activate the Facing Star. So if a Facing Star sees higher ground, big unmoving structures or a hill, it is de-activated. Similarly, if a Sitting Star, which is a Yin star, sees water, lower ground or a road junction, it will become de-activated.

Sometimes, it's not necessary to actually de-activate a star. If a star does not see the Forms it should see, but also does not see Forms that it should not see, then it is simply inactive. Just like the switches for the lights in your house are off by default. So generally, you need to be more conscious of Forms that activate or trigger a star, rather than those that de-activate a star.

玄
空
飛
星
風
水

# The Lights are On...

By this stage, you know how the Facing Stars and Sitting Stars are activated, based on the Form features outside the property. But knowing how to activate a star is one thing – you need to know what happens when you activate that particular star, right?

To determine whether the favourable or negative aspects of a star are activated, we have to look at whether or not the star is timely or not. If the star is timely, then its positive attributes will manifest. And so when you activate such a star, the positive aspects can be unlocked and utilised. By contrast, if a star is untimely, it will show its negative attributes when activated.

In case you have forgotten, the timeliness of a star is determined by looking at the present Period Luck. Currently, we are in Period 8, which runs from 2004-2023.

| Cycle | Period | Year | Gua | |
|---|---|---|---|---|
| 上<br>Upper | 1 | 1864 - 1883 | ☵ | 坎 Kan |
| | 2 | 1884 - 1903 | ☷ | 坤 Kun |
| | 3 | 1904 - 1923 | ☳ | 震 Zhen |
| 中<br>Middle | 4 | 1924 - 1943 | ☴ | 巽 Xun |
| | 5 | 1944 - 1963 | | - |
| | 6 | 1964 - 1983 | ☰ | 乾 Qian |
| 下<br>Lower | 7 | 1984 - 2003 | ☱ | 兌 Dui |
| | 8 | 2004 - 2023 | ☶ | 艮 Gen |
| | 9 | 2024 - 2043 | ☲ | 離 Li |

玄空飛星風水

| Period | Upper 上 | | | Middle 中 | | | Lower 下 | | |
|---|---|---|---|---|---|---|---|---|---|
| | 1 | 2 | 3 | 4 | 5 | 6 | 7 | 8 | 9 |
| 旺氣 Prosperous Qi | 1 | 2 | 3 | 4 | 5 | 6 | 7 | 8 | 9 |
| 生氣 Growing Qi | 2<br>3 | 3<br>4 | 4<br>5 | 5<br>6 | 6<br>7 | 7<br>8 | 8<br>9 | 9<br>1 | 1<br>2 |
| 退氣 Retreating Qi | 9 | 1 | 2 | 3 | 4 | 5 | 6 | 7 | 8 |
| 死氣 Dead Qi | 6<br>7 | 9<br>6 | 1<br>6 | 2<br>8 | 2<br>3 | 4<br>9 | 5<br>4<br>3 | 2<br>6 | 6<br>7 |
| 煞氣 Killing Qi | 5 | 5<br>7 | 7<br>9 | 7<br>9 | 2<br>9 | 2<br>3 | 2<br>3 | 3<br>4<br>5 | 3<br>4<br>5 |

Now, using the Period Luck table above, we can see that during Period 8, stars #8, #9 and #1 are timely. All other stars are either neutral or untimely.

Xuan Kong Flying Stars at its most basic level is simply about using the right method to activate the right star. And naturally, we only want to activate the timely and auspicious stars, and leave the untimely and inauspicious ones alone.

玄空飛星風水

Let me show you, using an example, how the activation of a star works and how to factor in the timeliness of the stars into the equation.

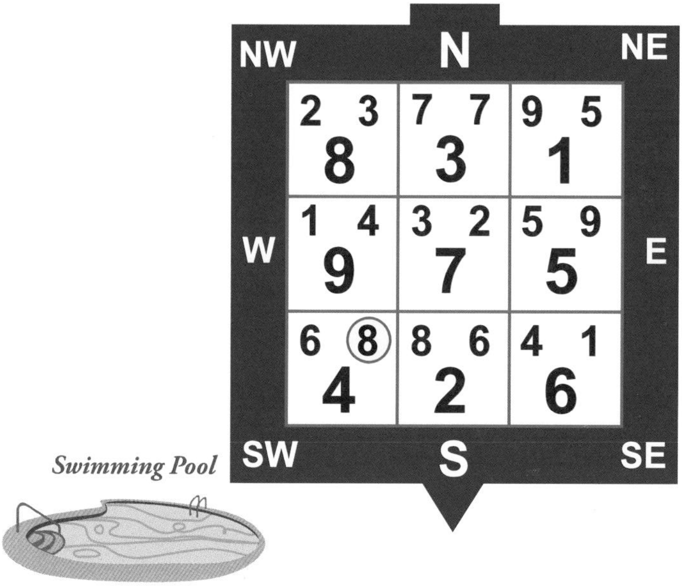

|  |  |  |
|---|---|---|
| NW | N | NE |

| 2 3<br>**8** | 7 7<br>**3** | 9 5<br>**1** |
|---|---|---|
| 1 4<br>**9** | 3 2<br>**7** | 5 9<br>**5** |
| 6 ⑧<br>**4** | 8 6<br>**2** | 4 1<br>**6** |

W — left side, E — right side

*Swimming Pool*    SW    S    SE

In this example, the property has water, in the form of a swimming pool, outside the #8 Facing Star location in the Southwest sector. As this #8 star is a Facing Star, and it is 'seeing' water, we can say this #8 star has been activated. Now, as the #8 is timely and is auspicious Qi in Period 8, we can say the #8 Facing Star in this property is activated and manifesting its positive qualities, which relate to wealth generation.

玄
空
飛
星
風
水

Let's try another example, this time using the #5 star.

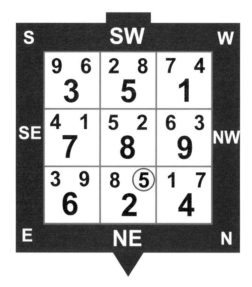

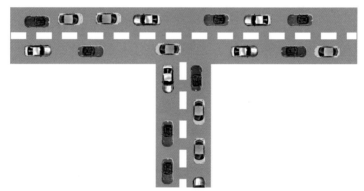

Outside the sector where the #5 Facing Star is located, there is a busy junction. Now, junctions as you have learnt earlier are Yang features. Facing Stars are activated by Yang features. So this #5 Facing Star is activated. However, the #5 is a negative star and it has been activated. Thus the negative aspects of the #5 Star will manifest.

Easy, right? Let's take things up a notch, by adding the interpretation layer.

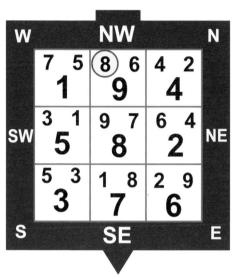

*When a Sitting Star sees a Yang form, it is known as a 'Mountain Dragon has Fallen into Water Formation'*

The #8 Sitting Star in this property sees Water, in the form of a pond, outside the palace that it resides in. Now, the Sitting Star is a Yin star, and so should not see an active Yang form like Water. We can say therefore the star is de-activated. The term for this kind of formation is "Mountain Dragon has Fallen into Water". The star that governs matters relating to family relations and people matters is now inside the Water. So what is the outcome of having such a formation?

There will be issues relating to fertility affecting the residents of this property and family relationships will also not be harmonious. Not that hard to figure out, right?

玄空飛星風水

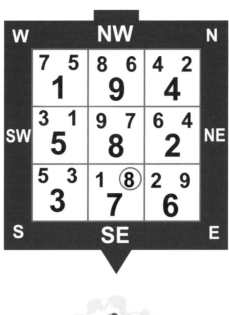

*When the Facing Star sees a Yin form, it is known as a 'Water Dragon goes up the Mountain Formation'*

So what if the situation is reversed? What if we have a #8 Facing Star with a hill immediately outside the palace where the #8 Facing Star is located? The #8 Facing Star should see a Yang form, but it now has become de-activated by the Yin form of the hill. This formation is known as "Water Dragon goes up the Mountain".

In this situation, the #8 Star, which governs Wealth matters, is weakened or completely ineffective. Accordingly the residents of the property will find making money an uphill slog, literally.

玄
空
飛
星
風
水

# Turn on the good stars, leave the bad stars alone

As beginners, you want to keep things simple for now. At this point, what you want is to get the basic principles right, and to be able to work with simple situations, before graduating on to the more complex scenarios.

Thus, your aim should be to activate the positive stars, using the right forms, and avoid activating the negative stars. The positive stars, as you know, are the stars that are timely and thus auspicious. The negative stars are the stars that are untimely and inauspicious.

As we are in Period 8, essentially using the timely positive stars means activating both the Facing and Sitting #8 Star using the right Forms, based on the type of star. This means the occupants of the property can reap both financial or wealth-related benefits, whilst also getting the people and health-related benefits.

玄
空
飛
星
風
水

As your knowledge of Xuan Kong Flying Stars becomes more advanced, I will show you how to add in more advanced concepts like the 'Right Star in the Right Palace' principle, which relates to exactly which kind of mountain form we want to see in which sector and Direct/Indirect Spirit rule which relates to the preferred location for Water forms outside the property. We will also add in star combinations, and also, learn how to classify a Natal chart by its structure.

As beginners, what matters is that you appreciate that Forms are integral to the activation and de-activation of the stars in a Natal chart, and the goal of Flying Stars Feng Shui is to simply activate the stars that are timely and auspicious, in order to gain the positive benefits of their energies.

Try this little exercise now. Take out the Natal chart of your own property and check what are the Forms you have outside the #8 Sitting and Facing Stars and then ask yourself if these stars are activated or de-activated by the Forms you see.

# The 3 Factors

By this stage, you will be able to look at a Natal chart and know what are the favourable stars and the unfavourable stars in a property. You are also aware of how these stars can be activated and how they can be de-activated, using Forms.

The next layer of understanding you must add is to be able to determine WHERE you want to see which stars.

Now, by where you want to see which stars, I mean, which areas of a residential property you want to make use of Sitting Stars, and where you want to make use of Facing Stars.

In the study of internal Feng Shui, not all rooms or areas of a property are created equal. As the emphasis in Feng Shui is to tap into the energies of the environment, to improve our quality of life, the focus naturally is on the areas that are most utilised in a home. There are three main areas that are always the focus of Feng Shui: the Main Door, the kitchen and the bedroom.

*Main Door*  *Kitchen*  *Bedroom*

玄
空
飛
星
風
水

# Understanding the 3 Factors

The Main Door obviously is important because this is the entrance to the property – in Feng Shui parlance, we call it the Qi mouth of the house. Whatever energies are in the environment enter the property through the Main Door.

Human beings need food for sustenance and need rest in order to repair and rejuvenate the body. Hence, Feng Shui pays close attention to how the kitchen and bedroom of a home are affected. Of course, these days, a person's career is an integral part of their lives. So increasingly, the focus is on the study or work areas in a home too. But the key basic areas are the Main Door, kitchen and bedroom, or what I call the Three Factors.

When we look at the Feng Shui of any property, we are interested in deriving a Qi map of the property (using Flying Stars for example) and then checking the Three Factors to see what energies are affecting these areas. Naturally, we want positive energies in all these three areas – that is a given.

More specifically, what kind of stars do you think we want to see in these areas? Naturally, we want to see all the stars that are timely and thus exuding prosperous Qi. Now, let's take it one step further. Which type of star (Sitting Star or Facing Star) do you think we activate in these areas?

# Stars at the Main Door

The Main Door is the doorway to the property. Hence, we naturally want it to be located in a sector with good stars. Now, in Period 8, the stars #8, #9 and #1 are timely and auspicious. Which star do we want to use?

Ideally, we want to use the most prosperous star. In every Period, the star of that Period is the most prosperous star. It is very important that you always take into account the timeliness of the stars. The current Period Luck, and the stars that are timely at this point in time, must always be taken into account when evaluating the Flying Stars in a property and whether or not an area has good or negative stars.

The dynamic changing nature of Qi is the key focus of Xuan Kong Flying Stars. So, we must consider what Qi is prosperous and auspicious now, and not what was prosperous and auspicious when the residents moved in. It does not matter WHEN you moved into the property or what Period Luck the chart has. We are interested in the here and now. Therefore, always focus on the stars that are timely and auspicious in the current period, and negative and untimely in the current period.

As we are now in Period 8 (2004 – 2023), the #8 Star is timely and prosperous. So, we want to have the Main Door in the palace where the #8 Star resides.

玄
空
飛
星
風
水

Now you're thinking – okay, I want the #8 but which #8? The Sitting or the Facing Star #8?

The Main Door is the doorway into a home. Think of how many people walk in and out of your home each day? Unless you enter your home by the back door, this is the entrance you use every day to go in and out of your home. Thus, a great deal of activity occurs at the Main Door area, which makes this area a Yang area, since Yang relates to movement and activity. What star is triggered by Yang activities? The Facing Star.

Thus, when it comes to the Main Door, the following principles are applied. Firstly, the Facing Star of the Palace where the Main Door is located is always what matters when it comes to the Main Door. Secondly, we want a timely and prosperous Facing Star where the Main Door is located.

玄
空
飛
星
風
水

Now, don't forget the Forms. Remember the mantra: *Forms activate the stars, stars in turn influence the Residents.* So, we also want to see Forms that support the Facing Star outside the palace where the Main Door is located. So water, a gently curving road, or lower ground are the types of forms that would support our Facing Star. If there are no supporting Yang forms, then at least, we don't want to see Yin forms, which will de-activate the Facing Star.

Let's take a look at an example to help you get the hang of things.

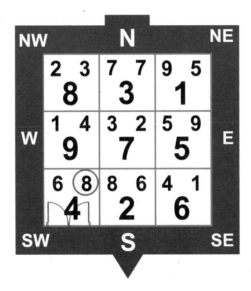

This is a Period 7 property, Facing South 2. The entrance to the house is located in the Southwest palace. As we are now in the year 2007 (at the time of writing) and it is Period 8, we pay attention to the stars that are timely and prosperous in Period 8. We DO NOT look at the stars that were timely and auspicious in Period 7, even though that is the Period Luck of the Natal chart.

玄
空
飛
星
風
水

This house opens a Main Door at the #8 Facing Star – in other words, the Main Door is sited where there is a prosperous wealth star. The Yang activity or movement of entering and exiting the house, and opening and closing the door, activates the #8 Facing Star.

The direction of the door is irrelevant. What matters is that is it located in the Southwest palace, where the #8 Facing Star is located.

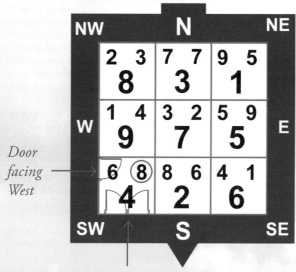

*It does not matter which way the door faces in this property. The important thing is there is a Door in the Southwest and the #8 Facing Star has been activated.*

玄空飛星風水

Now, let's change the dynamics of our scenario a little and see what we get.

| | | |
|---|---|---|
| **NW** | **N** | **NE** |
| 2 3<br>**8** | 7 7<br>**3** | 9 5<br>**1** |
| **W** 1 4<br>**9** | 3 2<br>**7** | 5 ⑨<br>**5** **E** |
| 6 8<br>**4** | 8 6<br>**2** | 4 1<br>**6** |
| **SW** | **S** | **SE** |

Here, the Main Door is not situated at the #8 star, but is located at the #9 Facing Star location. We still consider this scenario as a Main Door at the Wealth Star location, but the outcomes are different based on the timeliness of the stars in question. Now, we know the #8 star is the Wealth Star of the current period, thus represents money made at the present time. The #9 star is the future Wealth Star, as it will be the prosperous star in Period 9. Thus, the #9 star represents future wealth, or income derived from a long-term investment.

玄
空
飛
星
風
水

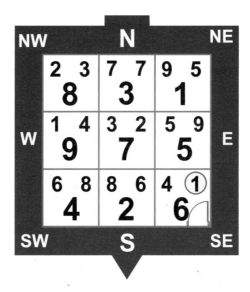

Let's tweak the scenario again. Now the door is in the Southeast, and activating the #1 Facing Star.

The #1 Star is the distant Wealth Star, thus it represent eventual wealth. As the #1 Star is the star of good name and reputation rather than actual wealth (see Chapter 6), we can also say a door in the palace with the #1 Facing Star also represents the residents of the property acquiring a good name and reputation in the future, building a good name and earning respect from peers and friends.

Now that you know what you're looking for at the palace where the Main Door is located, let's take a look at what stars we want to see in the bedroom and kitchen areas.

玄
空
飛
星
風
水

## Stars in the Bedroom

The bedroom, being an important aspect of the home where Feng Shui is concerned, is naturally also a place where we like to see timely and auspicious stars. So a #8, #9 or #1 star is ideal for a palace where the bedroom is located.

Now, the bedroom is where we sleep. Sleep is a Yin activity since Yin relates to stillness and non-movement. So therefore, we want to use a good Sitting Star for the bedroom. Remember Sitting Stars need to have Yin forms - so they should be in still and quiet rooms or rooms with little activity.

*The Northwest is an ideal place for the bedroom due to the presence of the Sitting Star #8.*

玄空飛星風水

The bedroom of a home therefore should ideally be located in a palace with a timely Sitting Star. This should be supported by appropriate Yin forms outside the palace, such as a hill, a mountain or higher ground. If there are no such forms, then we don't want to see Yang forms, as these would de-activate the Sitting Star.

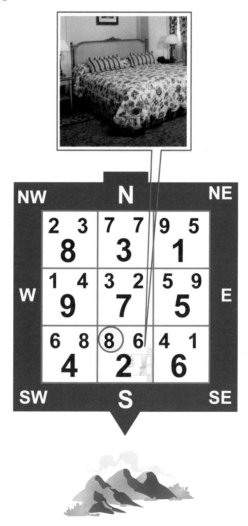

*A real mountain outside the South sector will support the Sitting Star #8 in this property., making the South room ideal as a bedroom.*

玄空飛星風水

It goes without saying that we do not want to sleep in a room with negative Sitting Stars so the bedroom should not be located in a palace where the #2, #3 and #5 star are located. These are not just the generally negative stars, but also stars that are not timely in the current Period.

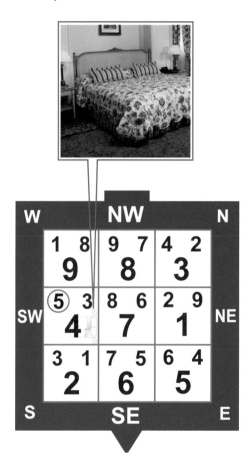

*In this example, the bedroom is located in a room with the #5 Sitting Star, which is a negative star. This bedroom is therefore not a good bedroom to use.*

玄
空
飛
星
風
水

## Stars in the Kitchen

The kitchen is where we cook and prepare food that we eat. Accordingly, this must be located in a sector with good stars (the #8, #9 or #1 star in Period 8), otherwise, cooking disasters won't be the only problem faced by the occupants. Cooking obviously is a Yang activity, so the Facing Star is the star that we pay attention to. Again, we want to see the appropriate Forms supporting the Facing Star in the kitchen.

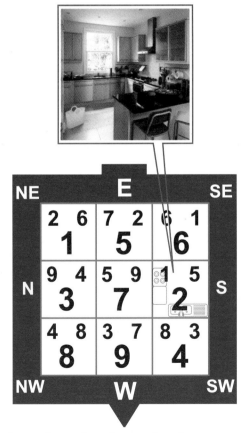

*The kitchen is located in the South palace, activating the negative #5 Facing Star. This is considered a bad location for the kitchen.*

玄
空
飛
星
風
水

Some flexibility is afforded to the stars found in the palace where the kitchen is located. Since people now do not always cook as much as they did in the old days, it is acceptable to locate the kitchen in a place with positive Sitting Stars as well. This is especially the case if the residents of the home are not of domestic goddess inclinations! However, typically, irrespective of whether or not the family cooks in the kitchen frequently or not, we usually prefer the Facing Star in the kitchen first, before resorting to using the Sitting Star.

It is also acceptable for the kitchen to have neutral stars, meaning, stars that are not necessarily timely, but are not negative, such as the #4 star. The #3 Star is also acceptable because the wood element is used to support the fire element of the stove. Some Flying Stars schools prefer to position the stove in the #3 and #4 Star location.

玄空飛星風水

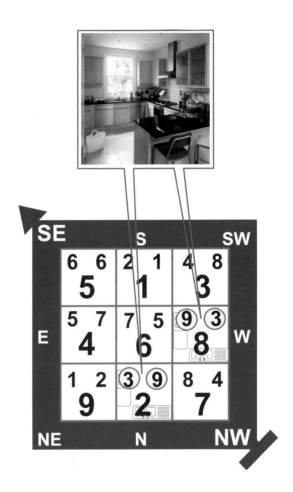

The North is a suitable location for the kitchen in this property,
as the #9 Facing Star is located here and there is the #3 Sitting
Star to provide supporting Wood Qi. The kitchen can also be
located in the West palace, where the #3 Facing Star is located,
and where there is also a good #9 Sitting Star.

玄
空
飛
星
風
水

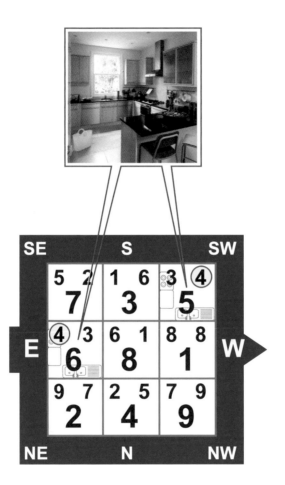

*In this example, the kitchen can be located either in the East palace or the Southwest palace, where the #4 Facing or Sitting Star is located.*

玄空飛星風水

However, you definitely do not want to have your kitchen located in a palace that contains the #2, #7 and #5. Sometimes, it is not possible to avoid a negative star in which case, it is best not to locate the kitchen in a palace where the Facing Star is negative. Look at the examples below:

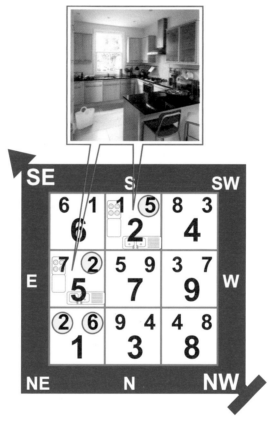

*In this example, the Northeast and East palaces are not suitable for the kitchen. The East has a #2 Facing Star whilst the Northeast has a #6 Facing Star. #6 star is the element of Metal so is not suitable for the kitchen as it is countered by Fire. Also, there is a #2 Sitting is in the Northeast as well. We also don't want the kitchen in the South, where the Facing Star #5, a negative star, is located.*

玄
空
飛
星
風
水

*The kitchen should not be located in the Northeast or South palaces of this property. Of the two palaces, the Northeast is the more detrimental palace as the Facing Star in this palace is the #2. The South palace looks usable, as the #1 Facing Star is located here. But as it comes with the #2 as the Sitting Star, it should be avoided as the #2 is the star of illness.*

In essence, aim to locate the kitchen in a sector with timely and auspicious stars or good stars. At all times, avoid having a negative star in the palace where the kitchen is to be located.

Flying Stars is not that hard, once you know what to look for, and where to look for it!

玄
空
飛
星
風
水

# Trouble-shooting Flying Stars

Naturally the scenarios discussed above are 'ideal' scenarios. Invariably, you will find that in many instances, one of these three factors is located in an inappropriate palace, or making use of the wrong star.

The answer is not to wring your hands, and bemoan your fate. I always say to my students: don't let what you can't do, stop you from doing what you can do. And when it comes to Feng Shui, at all times, we should strive to make use of whatever areas we can, rather than feel restricted by the limitations of the property.

As a Feng Shui consultant, my job is to try to help my clients make use of what is available. Any consultant can say a property is bad or has the 3 factors located in the wrong place. That is what I call 'kindergarten' Flying Stars. The mark of a good practitioner is one who can offer workable solutions.

So, what are some of the options available when things are not all peachy when it comes to the location of the Main Door, bedroom or kitchen in a given property?

The answer is essentially in the understanding of what activates and de-activates the stars, and an appreciation of the timeliness of the stars.

Let's run through a few typical scenarios and I'll show you how to think your way out of the problem.

玄
空
飛
星
風
水

**Problem: Main Door is not located in a palace with the prosperous Facing Star**

Solution: In Period 8, there are 3 stars that are timely and auspicious – the #8, the #9 and the #1. All in all, you have 3 stars to play with. If you can't get the door at Facing #8, then what about the Facing #9 or Facing #1? See – plenty of options as long as one is not pigheaded about the situation. Remember, Qi has a dynamic nature and nothing is permanent. And having future wealth may not be as good as current wealth, but it is better than no wealth surely?

**Problem: Main Door cannot be located in #8, #9 or #1 Facing Stars**

Solution: Again, all is not doomed. You can still make use of the #8 Facing Stars by utilising your knowledge of activating stars. Usually, Feng Shui practitioners will activate the star through natural means. What does this mean? The advanced method is to use the natural formations (mountains and water) outside the property. A more simple (but no less effective) method is to simply make appropriate use of the palace where the favourable stars are located.

Now, we know Facing Stars are triggered by Yang activities. So if you can't put a door where the good stars are located, use the room where the good stars are located, for Yang activities such as a study, a workroom or just a living room where you watch television. If you want to use the Sitting Star, use the room for resting, meditation or as a quiet place to read and relax.

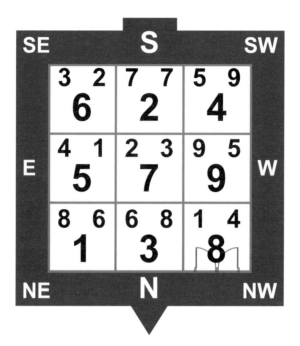

| SE | S | SW |
|---|---|---|
| 3 2 **6** | 7 7 **2** | 5 9 **4** |
| 4 1 **5** | 2 3 **7** | 9 5 **9** |
| 8 6 **1** | 6 8 **3** | 1 4 **8** |

E — W

NE  N  NW

*In this Period 7, North 1 facing property, the door is not located in a favourable palace. But there is a pond in the North sector where the #8 Facing Star is located. This natural water activates the #8 Facing Star.*

玄
空
飛
星
風
水

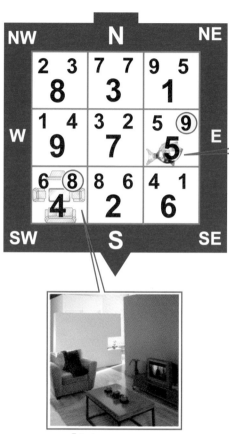

*Aquarium*

*Living room*

To make use of the positive and timely stars in this property, we locate the living room, where the family spends time, in the Southwest palace. Activity triggers the #8 Facing Star. Water, in the form of an aquarium, is placed in the East palace, where the #9 Facing Star is located. Thus, two timely and positive stars are activated in this property, with minimal change and alteration.

玄空飛星風水

If this is not workable for some reason, then we resort to some artificial means to trigger the positive stars. Water is classified as Yang so placing an aquarium in the room where the positive stars are located is a simple but effective means to help activate the star. This should also ideally be supported by external water such as a fish pond.

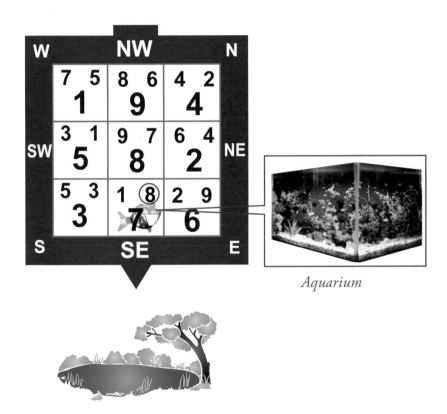

*Aquarium*

*An aquarium is used to activate the #8 Facing Star at the Southeast Palace. It would be ideal of there is also natural water, in the form of a pond, outside the Southeast Palace.*

玄
空
飛
星
風
水

## Problem: what do I do with the #2 and #5?

Solution: The first rule when it comes to Feng Shui is to always try to avoid a situation rather than forcefully resolve it. This is especially the case with the #5 Yellow Star. Prevention is always better than cure. If any of your 3 Factors is located at the #2 or #5 stars, be it Facing or Sitting, you need to see if there are any options or alternatives available. For example, if the Main Door triggers the #2 or #5 Facing Star, consider using a side door or back door. If the bedroom triggers the Sitting #2 or #5, sleeping in another bedroom may be the answer.

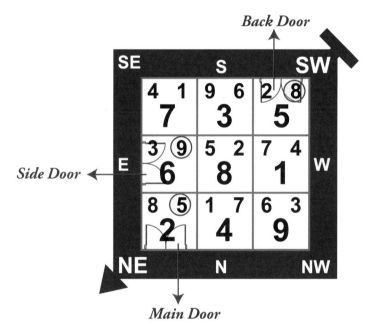

*Main Door*

*This house has a Main Door at the Northeast sector, where the #5 Facing Star is located. However, the house also has an East side door, located where the #9 Facing Star is and a Southwest back door where the #8 Facing Star is located. Solution — use the side door or back door more often or as the main means of entry into the property.*

玄
空
飛
星
風
水

If none of these options are feasible, then you may still be able to reduce the effects of the #5 if it is not triggered by external forms. Check to see if the Sitting #5 is triggered by any Yin forms outside the bedroom. If the star is not triggered by external forms, then you have a zero-sum gain situation – which in Feng Shui, is not always a bad thing. A neutral situation is always better than an unfavourable situation.

*This property has a bedroom in the Southeast sector. Both the Sitting and Facing Stars in this room are negative stars. It is best to avoid using this bedroom if possible. However, if the #5 is not triggered by external forms, then this room may still be usable.*

玄空飛星風水

The #5 Star is weakened by Metal. If there is an activated #5 Star in the bedroom, place sports trophies or pewter ware or silverware in a shelf in the bedroom or utilise a bed with a metal frame.

You may have noticed that I have not mentioned anything about 'suppressing' the negative stars. This is a common approach with Eight Mansions Feng Shui (Ba Zhai Feng Shui) but is what differentiates Xuan Kong Flying Stars from Eight Mansions. This is not to say that Eight Mansions contradicts Flying Stars – in fact, the two systems can be used in tandem by a Feng Shui practitioner. Rather, this simply shows how different Feng Shui systems have different approaches. As long as you practice the different systems separately and don't try to mix things up, there is no problem.

What we have discussed here are simple and basic practical solutions to some of the common problems. As you advance, we will look at using principles such as the small Tai-Ji technique, placement of beds and desks to make a bad room usable, Combinations and Structures to resolve situations. As you advance in your understanding of Xuan Kong Feng Shui, you will begin to see that classical Feng Shui does not involve the placement of objects or curing as the first line of defence against a problematic situation.

玄
空
飛
星
風
水

# Going forward...

By this stage, you already have the knowledge and skills needed to undertake the audit of a house. You are able to plot a Flying Stars chart to establish the Qi map of the property. You are able to determine which are the favourable and unfavourable areas of a property by determining where the timely and untimely stars are located. You also know what stars you want to see, in which areas of the house, based on the 3 Factors of Main Door, bedroom and kitchen. Through the understanding of how to activate the stars, you also know how specific areas of a property should be used and which rooms should not be used. You would also have some basic knowledge of Forms and how these influence the stars in a property.

All these are, in effect, what a stand-alone Flying Stars Feng Shui consultation entails and involves. Of course, you're not quite ready to go out and practice as a consultant but you're certainly well-equipped to audit your own house and undertake some modest changes to improve the Feng Shui of your own property, with no renovation cost!

*The 3 Factors: Main Door, Bedroom and Kitchen.*

玄
空
飛
星
風
水

*A good main door location, receives positive Qi for the entire house.*

Xuan Kong Feng Shui, like any other Chinese Metaphysical study, involves increasing layers of complexity and sophistication. I believe it is important to get people off the ground and able to do something (such as analyse their own house) early on. Never underestimate the value of a simple approach and just using the basics is what I always tell my students.

But at the same time, it is important to be aware that there is much, much more about Xuan Kong Feng Shui that goes beyond just the mere basics. And in the next chapter, I am going to share with you some of these more advanced ideas and concepts, and some of the more sophisticated solutions typically used in Xuan Kong Feng Shui (often considered trade secrets) by showing you how a professional Feng Shui consultant would audit a property using Xuan Kong Feng Shui.

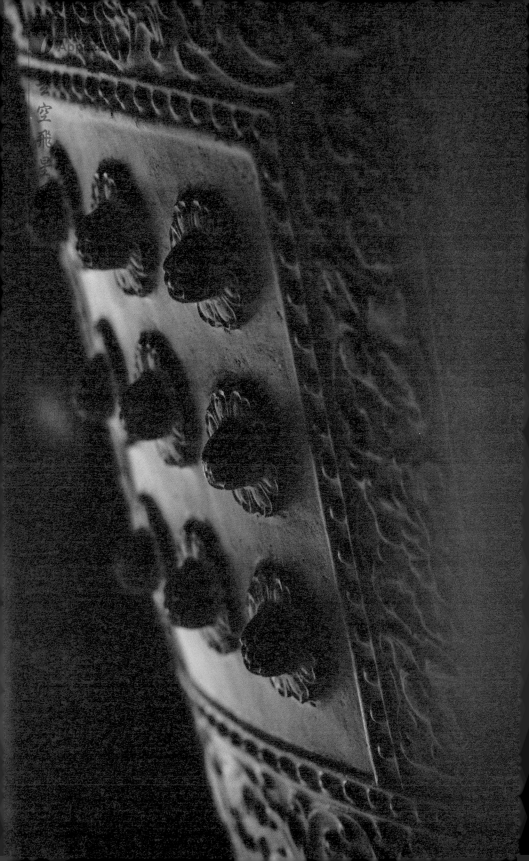

# Chapter 8:
# Practical Application of Xuan Kong Flying Stars

玄空飛星風水

玄
空
飛
星
風
水

Learning Flying Stars is not hard. But the application of Flying Stars, including the ability to solve problems, is what distinguishes a practitioner from a student. As a Feng Shui consultant, my job is not just to tell clients what's wrong and what's bad about their property (that's easy), but to also provide them with a solution to their problems. Not just any solution. A solution that is not costly to undertake (massive renovation is not the preferred choice of most clients), and is practical, but at the same time, one that is effective, with results that can be seen as soon as possible! Yes, being a Feng Shui consultant or practitioner is more than just about pronouncing a property as 'bad'.

That is why I have included this chapter. There is no better way to understand the application of Flying Stars, and also learn how to think your way through a Flying Stars problem, than by seeing how it is done. Now, some more advanced concepts like Combinations will be touched on here, and I will also be talking about the technique known as 'Small Tai-Ji'. Do not worry if it goes over your head right now. The idea is for you to be aware that there are more advanced concepts ahead and also, to see how Xuan Kong has many techniques, beyond just placing water or hanging wind chimes, to improve the Feng Shui of a property.

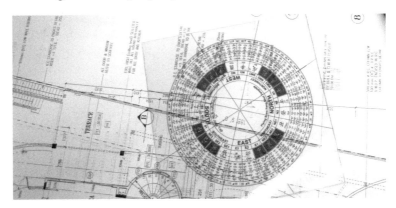

玄
空
飛
星
風
水

I have chosen 3 examples here: an apartment, a linked house and a double storey bungalow house. I will walk you through the examples step by step, from plotting the chart to analysing the chart. I will also show you how a professional Feng Shui consultant would make adjustments to the property or recommend changes to room usage to tap into the positive stars, minimise the impact of the negative stars and utilise as many of the rooms in the property as possible.

The analysis of all these charts is done based on Period 8. It is important to note this because that means that in Period 9, the analysis of these properties will not be the same as the Period Luck affecting these properties has changed.

*Apartment*

*Linked House*

*Bungalow*

玄空飛星風水

## The Apartment

The apartment that we will be auditing has a W1 facing and is a Period 8 building. Here is the Natal chart for a Period 8, W1 facing building.

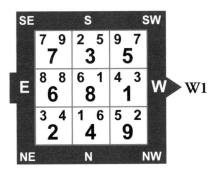

Here is the floor plan of the apartment unit.

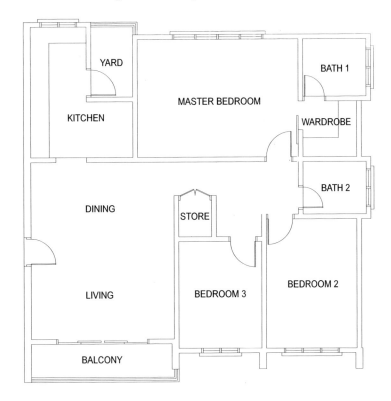

玄
空
飛
星
風
水

# Pre-Audit Preparation

A good Feng Shui practitioner always does the homework before proceeding to the analysis.

### Step 1: Divide the apartment unit using the 9 Grids

You should also mark out the Palace directions for easy reference. To do this, you just need to know the North and South axis of the unit - stand in the middle of the apartment with a compass or stand on the balcony to determine the North palace.

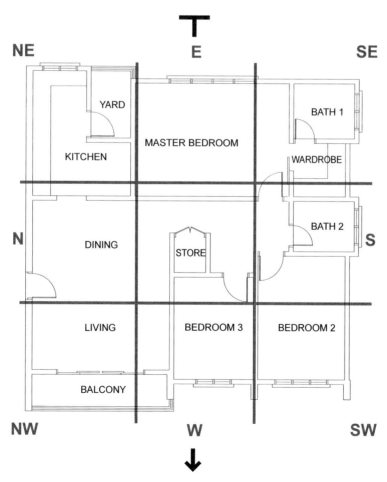

玄空飛星風水

## Step 2: Super-impose the Natal Chart on the apartment floor plan

Transfer the stars according to the palace they reside in from the Natal chart.

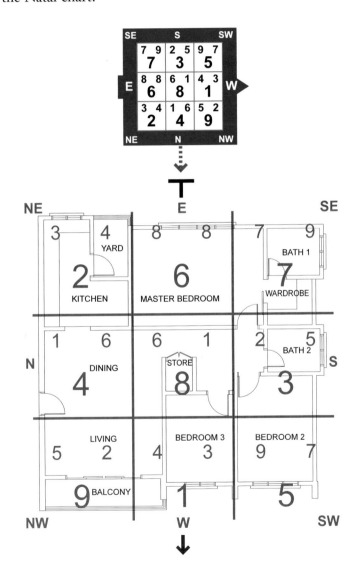

# Feng Shui Analysis

I'm going to run 2 levels of analysis: the first level is a basic analysis, using the information and techniques that you have learnt from Chapter 2 to Chapter 7 of this book. The 2nd level of analysis will be a little more advanced.

## Basic Flying Stars Analysis

Let's zero in on the 3 factors because these are the most important aspects of any property that we want to analyse. We'll start with the Main Door.

This apartment unit has its Main Door in the North sector, and so it is activating the #6 Facing Star. Remember we always look at the Facing Star when it comes to the Main Door as the Main Door area is regarded as Yang and active.

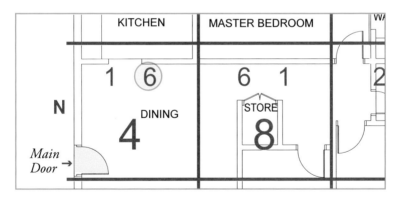

From previous chapters, we know that the #6 is not a very prosperous star in Period 8 but it is not a bad star by nature either. Remember what I said about how in Feng Shui a zero-sum gain situation is not necessarily a bad thing? So in this case, that is what we have. The Main Door is not fantastic but it is also not bad. It's an average Main Door. The occupants of this property will be able to acquire wealth but it will be through steady hard work and usually via employment.

Now, let's take a look at the bedrooms. There are 3 bedrooms in this property. The Master Bedroom is in the East palace, Bedroom 2 and Bedroom 3 are in the Southwest and West palaces respectively. Now, remember with the bedrooms, we are looking at the Sitting Stars primarily.

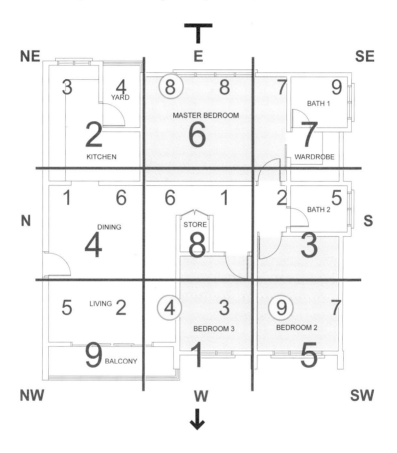

The Master Bedroom makes use of the #8 Sitting Star. This is ideal because the #8 is the most prosperous star of Period 8 and so we want to use it as much as possible. Also, this is a bedroom, using the #8 Sitting Star means relationships between the couple occupying the master bedroom will definitely be smooth and good. The occupants will also have no problems with their work relationships or health problems.

玄
空
飛
星
風
水

Bedroom 2 is using the #9 Sitting Star which is one of the timely stars in Period 8. So, Bedroom 2 is fine. Bedroom 3 makes use of the #4 Sitting Star. #4 in itself is not a bad star but it is not timely in Period 8 so this room is not so good as a bedroom. Now you might be wondering: what about the academic attributes associated with the #4? Surely this room would be suitable as a bedroom for a school-going child since they could still get the academic benefits from the #4? Studying is a Yang activity and so would involve the use of the Facing Star rather than the Sitting Star. However since the governing star for this bedroom is a Sitting Star #4, which governs people, this does indicate that the child in this room will have academic progress as Sitting Stars exert an influence on people matters.

Bedroom 3 is also not so good because the combination of stars in the room, which is #4-#3 combination, is a combination that denotes arguments and rebelliousness. The visual image of this combination is two sticks hitting each other. However, if there is a quiet child in the family, then this room could be usable by that child because it would make the child speak up more and become more outgoing.

玄空飛星風水

Finally, what about the kitchen? The kitchen is located in a sector with a favourable star, which is the #4. It's not a timely star but it's suitable for a kitchen as it is a Wood star, and Wood supports the Fire element that is associated with cooking

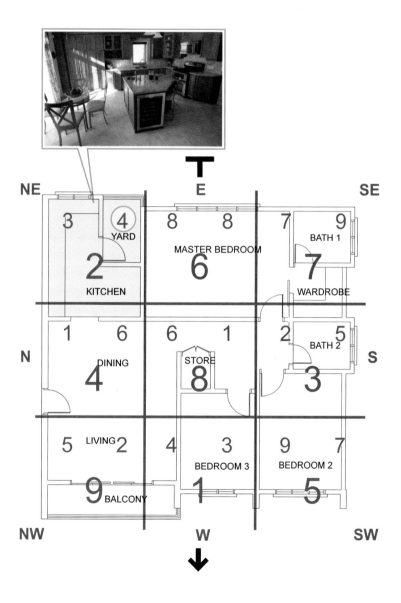

玄空飛星風水

Now, what about the #5 Star? The Facing #5 is located in bathroom 2 so is harmless and not a cause for concern as this is not an important room. The other #5 Star is at the living room. This is not so good but is easily fixed. Have the residents place all their pewter ware, silverware and sports trophies in the living room, and the metal will weaken the #5 Star.

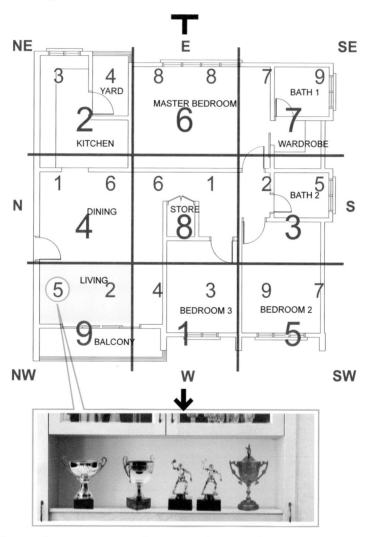

See – that was easy right? Now, let me show you how we would analyse this apartment using some advanced principles and techniques.

玄空飛星風水

## Advanced Flying Stars Analysis

Now, when we analyse this property using advanced Xuan Kong Flying Stars, this property actually has quite a good door. North is the Indirect Spirit sector, according to the Direct-Indirect Spirit principle and is suitable to see Yang activity such as a door or water. Also, this chart has a 1-6 combination, known as a He Tu Water combination at the Main Door, denoting academic and sporting success, and wealth acquired through partnerships or ventures with other people. If this house also has natural water outside the North sector, this would be ideal.

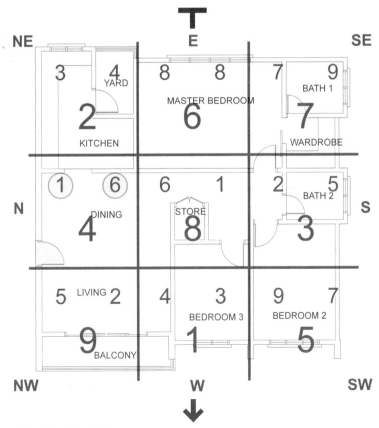

玄
空
飛
星
風
水

Let's throw in the Combinations and the Small Tai-Ji technique to see how we can further refine and improve the Feng Shui of these rooms.

The Small Tai-Ji technique involves simply dividing up the room into a further 9 Grids, and then evaluating the room, in the same way one would evaluate the house or apartment unit. This is an important technique for fine-tuning the Feng Shui of specific rooms through the placement of the beds and study or work desks in a bedroom.

*Using the Small Tai-Ji in Master Bedroom*

The challenge in the Master Bedroom would be to make use of both the #8 stars. This is where the Small Tai-Ji technique is very handy. The Master Bedroom has the double 8 combination – most books will tell you that this means you have to 'sacrifice' one of the stars, either the Sitting Star or Facing Star. With the Small Tai-Ji technique, this is not necessary. It just means the master bedroom has to double up as both a sleeping and work area.

玄空飛星風水

In the case of the Master bedroom, we want to place the bed either on the 1-6 or the bed in the 8-8. Then the work desk can be placed either in the 8-8 (if 1-6 is used for the bed) or the 1-6 (if the 8-8 is used for the bed). Now, the occupant of the Master Bedroom can tap into both the current Wealth Star and also the #1 Sitting Star.

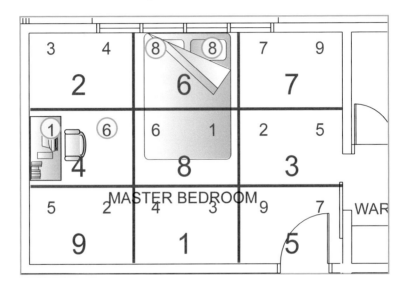

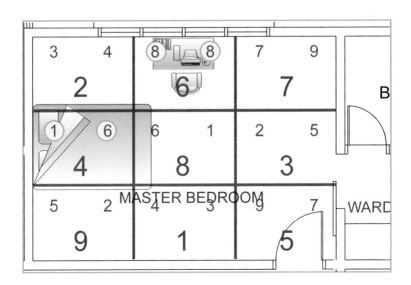

玄空飛星風水

Bedroom 2 has a 9-7 combination and this is regarded as a combination that is favourable for romance luck so this is a good room to locate a single adult. The room itself is good to begin with, using the #9 Sitting Star when we look at the apartment unit as a whole. So we would just want to position the bed back in the same sector, using the Small Tai-Ji technique.

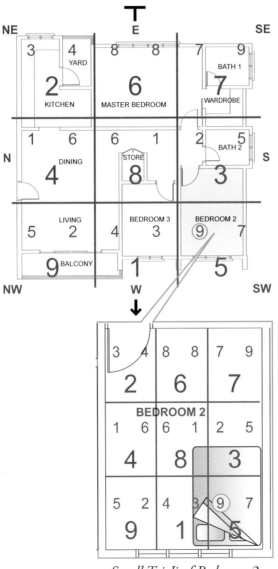

*Small Tai-Ji of Bedroom 2*

The kitchen is already using a favourable star in the macro-picture. So now, we just want to use the Small Tai-Ji technique to position the stove, at the 3-4 stars.

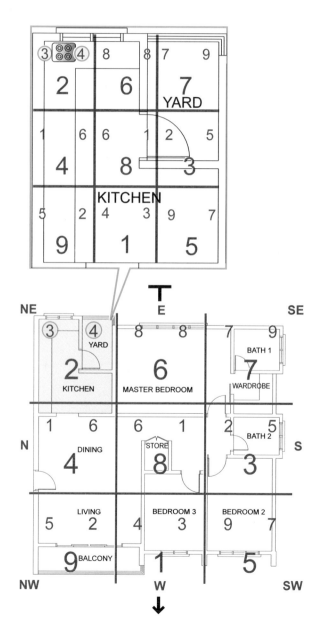

At the advanced level, we will also want to try to unlock and tap into as many of the timely stars as possible. One of the problems that would appear to be present in this property is the Facing Star #9 is in the bathroom of the Master Bedroom in the Southeast sector. This is an easy fix. Remember Facing Stars are activated by water? All the residents need to do is install a bathtub in the bathroom and use it more often! This not just activates the #9 Facing Star but also conforms with the Direct/Indirect Spirit principle. So the occupants can literally make money while in the bath tub!

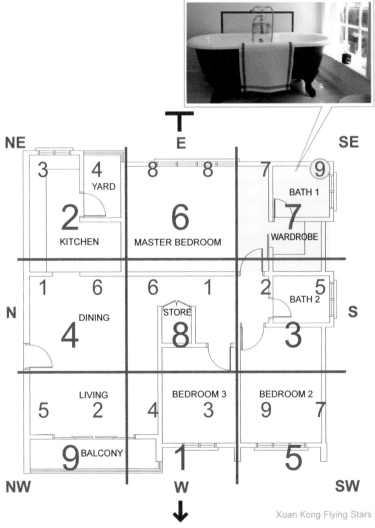

玄空飛星風水

## Double Storey Linked House

The 2nd property that we will be auditing has a S2 facing and is a Period 7 building – the owners moved into the new house in 2002, making this house a Period 7 building. Here is the Natal chart for a Period 7, S2 facing building. This house is to be occupied by 4 occupants. They would like to know if this property has good Feng Shui or not.

**S2**

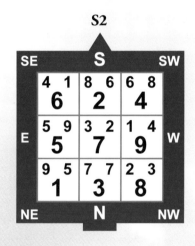

| SE | S | SW |
|---|---|---|
| 4 1 <br> **6** | 8 6 <br> **2** | 6 8 <br> **4** |
| 5 9 <br> **5** | 3 2 <br> **7** | 1 4 <br> **9** |
| 9 5 <br> **1** | 7 7 <br> **3** | 2 3 <br> **8** |

(E on left, W on right; NE bottom-left, N bottom-centre, NW bottom-right)

玄空飛星風水

Here is the floor plan of the double storey linked house.

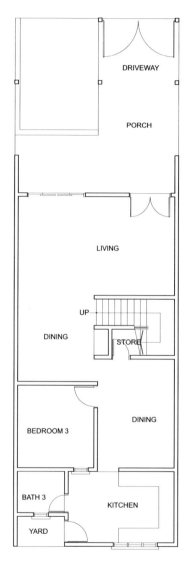

GROUND FLOOR PLAN

1ST FLOOR PLAN

玄空飛星風水

# Pre-Audit Preparation

Super-imposing the Natal chart onto this house is slightly easier because you already know which part of the house corresponds with the structure. However, a little more work is required because you have to super-impose the Natal chart on BOTH the ground floor and the 1st floor of the house.

## Step 1: Divide the house using the 9 Grids

Mark out the Palace directions for easy reference.

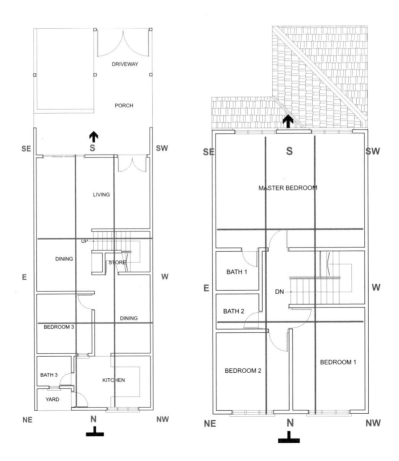

玄
空
飛
星
風
水

## Step 2: Super-impose the Natal Chart on the house floor plan

Transfer the Flying Stars from the Natal Chart into the house floor plan. Remember, transfer the Flying Stars to both the ground floor and the 1st floor plans. A few things to note here: firstly, the floor plan also shows the driveway to this property. We do not expand the 9 Grids to include the driveway because this is not a living space. Secondly, this is an elongated property, so we will stretch the grids a little to ensure we get all 9 Palaces represented in the property.

You may have also noticed that this property has a Main Door that is also the same direction of the Facing. Therefore, the area marked (X) is where you would normally stand to take a direction.

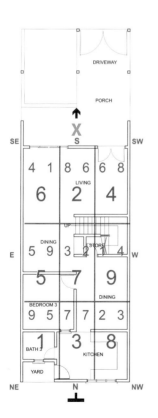

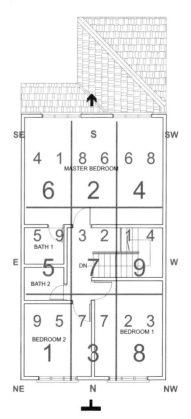

玄
空
飛
星
風
水

# Feng Shui Analysis

### Basic Flying Stars Analysis

We begin our analysis by looking at the 3 Factors: the Main Door, the bedroom and the kitchen. Now, we are interested in the quality of the star at the Main Door – so look at the floor plan for the ground floor of this property, specifically the Main Door. What stars do we see?

This house has a #8 Facing Star at the Main Door. In Period 8, the #8 Star is prosperous and denotes good wealth opportunities. So, we say this house has a good Wealth Door and receives prosperous Qi.

Remember, the Period Luck of the house itself, which is Period 7, is not what concerns us at this point. We are only interested in the stars that are timely and auspicious presently in Period 8. There's no need for the owner of this property to 'do anything' to their Main Door or activate the #8 Facing Star because as long as they are using the Main Door as the entrance to their property, they are activating the #8 Facing Star.

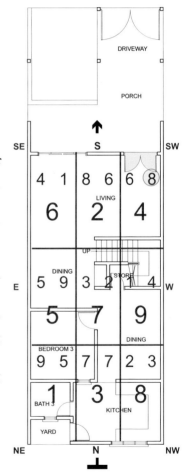

Let's move to the bedroom on the ground floor, labeled Bedroom 3 on the floor plan. This bedroom is located in the third quadrant of the house, near the back of the property, so we look at the Northeast palace for the stars that govern this room. Although the grids cut the room in half, remember the 9 Grids are to give you an estimation only of the way the Qi is distributed in the property.

Whilst I don't suggest you get 'creative' with how the Qi and stars are allocated – certainly, wavering the line, because you don't like the fact that some good stars happen to be located in the toilet, is being creative. But you also shouldn't be too rigid either, especially when you are looking at houses with long Qi, such as this one. As most of the room is near the back and only a small portion is in the center section of the house, the stars in the Northeast palace govern Bedroom 3.

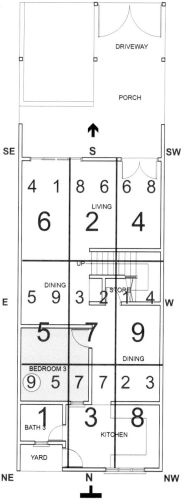

Now because it is a bedroom, we are mostly looking at the Sitting Stars. This bedroom is using the #9 Sitting Star. This is a good star in Period 8 and so we can say Bedroom 3 is correctly located and tapping into a good star and thus, is a good bedroom. Don't let the #5 Facing Star in Bedroom 3 panic you. Remember, we're using this room as a Bedroom and the #5 Yellow here is the Facing Star. So as long as this room is also not used for work but is purely used for sleeping, the #5 remains inactive, assuming there are no forms that activate the #5 Facing Star outside the Northeast Palace.

Typically in a double storey house, the elderly members of the family usually use the downstairs bedroom as it is less difficult for them to access the bedroom when it is downstairs. Since most seniors are not interested in making money and are more focused on good health, Bedroom 3 is ideal for a senior member of the family to sleep in.

Let's move to the bedrooms upstairs. The Master Bedroom straddles 3 palaces but you will notice most of the 'good' stars are located in this room. So we know the Master Bedroom is a pretty good bedroom.

However, this room also presents a small problem because of the internal forms. If we want the occupants to use the #8 Sitting Star by placing their bed there using the Small Tai-Ji technique, then the bed is necessarily located in front of the door to the Master Bedroom. If you have read my book, *Feng Shui for Homebuyers - Interiors*, you will note that this is not a favourable Internal Form to have in the bedroom, as the Qi from the door crashes right into the bed.

玄空飛星風水

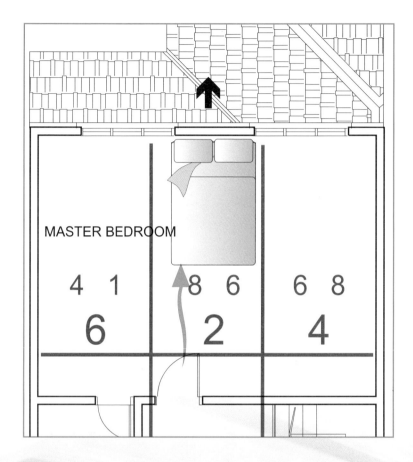

MASTER BEDROOM

4 1
6

8 6
2

6 8
4

*Qi from the door, crashes straight into the bed, if the bed is placed in the 8-6 star position, using the Small Tai-Ji technique*

玄
空
飛
星
風
水

This is however not a really difficult problem. The owners can do a few things: first, they can renovate the property and have the door to the bedroom moved to the right but this may not be possible due to the location of the staircase. Furthermore, as I have indicated in ***Feng Shui for Homebuyers - Interiors***, from an Internal Forms standpoint, we do not like there to be a tight space between the staircase and the bedroom door. We like the bedroom door to have a spacious area in front of it to serve as a little Mini-Bright Hall 明堂(Ming Tang)

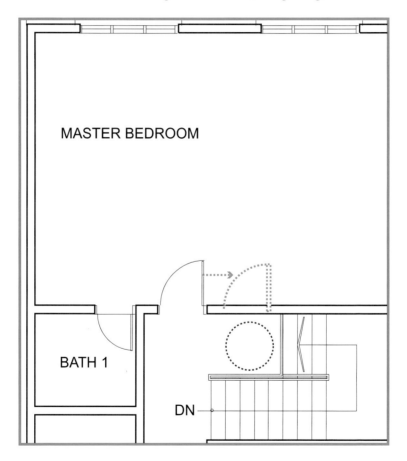

*If the door to the Master Bedroom is moved, the space in front of the door becomes tight and constricted and there is no Mini-Bright Hall in front of the bedroom door. Qi has no place to collect.*

玄
空
飛
星
風
水

Therefore, the only option is to place a screen the length of the door, in front of the door. This way, the bed can be positioned at the Sitting Star #8. The work desk can then be placed either in the Facing #8 Star location or the Facing #1 Star location, using the Small Tai-Ji technique. Which position the Feng Shui consultant chooses will depend largely on the needs of the client. The 4-1 combination is better for creative fields, marketing and public relations or those engaged in educational businesses. The 6-8 would favour a client who is an entrepreneur or a corporate person.

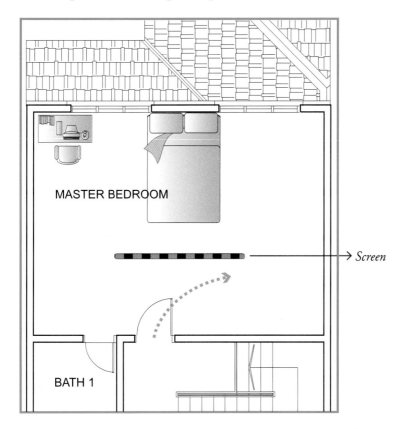

*Place a screen in front of the bedroom door, to prevent the Qi from crashing into the bed.*

玄
空
飛
星
風
水

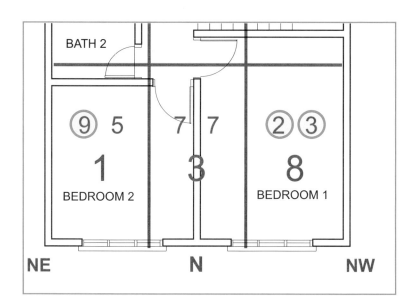

Bedroom 1 is definitely not a good bedroom, with no usable stars – both the #2 and #3 are negative stars so the room is not usable for sleeping or working. Anyone sleeping in this room will have lots of arguments with the people around them as, in advanced Xuan Kong Flying Stars, #2 and #3 together forms a combination known as Bullfight Sha, denoting lots of arguments and disputes. So, it is advisable this bedroom is not used.

Bedroom 2 is a better room because the Sitting Star #9 can be used. Since this property only has 4 occupants, it is possible for Bedroom 1 to be left empty or used to store items.

Now, let's check the kitchen. The kitchen is located right at the back of the property and would appear to straddle two palaces. When a room appears to span two palaces, we use the corner to determine which stars apply to the room. As the corner of the kitchen is located in the Northwest sector, so we reference the stars in the Northwest sector to determine the quality of the Flying Stars in the kitchen. Here, the kitchen is located in what seems to be an unfavorable 2-3 Bullfight Sha combination. However, as this is the kitchen, the Facing Star #3, being a Wood element star, is acceptable for a Kitchen. So there's really no need to do anything with the kitchen.

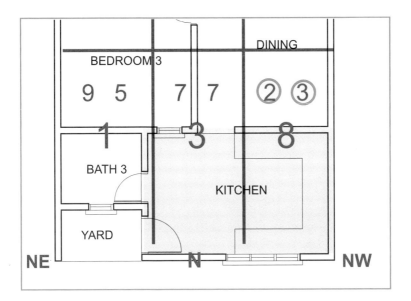

Using our basic analysis of the Flying Stars of this property, we can conclude that this property generally has good Feng Shui, with the exception of Bedroom 1 upstairs.

玄空飛星風水

## Advanced Flying Stars Analysis

A more advanced analysis of this property will entail going down to the specifics of each of the 3 Factors and also, looking to see how we can use techniques like the Small Tai-Ji technique to improve the quality of Qi. We also want to use more advanced techniques to refine the quality of the Feng Shui in each room to make it more effective. A more advanced analysis will also look at the location of the staircase as this is the means in which the Qi travels to the upper level of the property.

Let's start downstairs.

We already know from our basic analysis that the Main Door is correctly located. In an advanced analysis, we also look at the external and internal forms. The Main Door, although located in a good palace, and activating the #8 Facing Star, has an unfavourable form outside.

Notice how the driveway and main gate are in direct alignment with the Main Door. This creates a mild Sha Qi (I say mild because the distance between the gate and the Main Door is not a great distance) but is still not something we want affecting the Main Door, which is the Qi Mouth of the property.

玄
空
飛
星
風
水

*Notice how the gate is aligned in a straight line with the Main*
*Door? This creates a negative form, known as Sha Qi.*

玄
空
飛
星
風
水

In this case, I would recommend the owner either move the driveway, or build a speed-bump that will slow the straightline movement of the Qi and make the Sha Qi less piercing. With favourable forms and a good Main Door, the Qi mouth to this property is pretty good already.

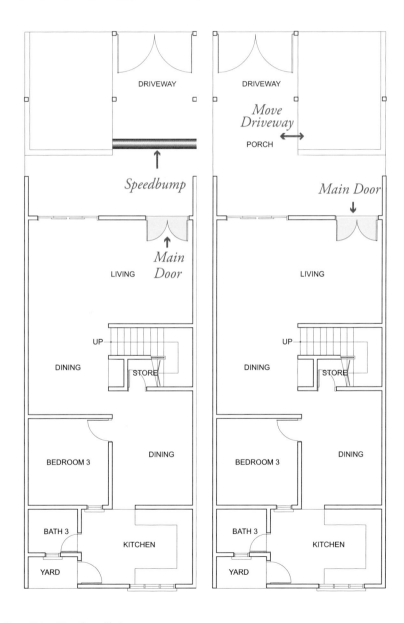

玄空飛星風水

We can also position a water feature in the SW sector. This serves to slow down the direct Qi clashing in from the main gate. Water also helps activate the Facing Star #8.

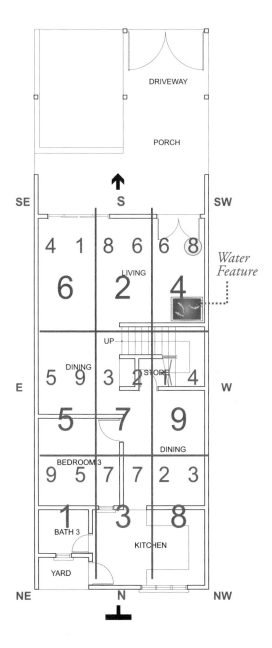

玄
空
飛
星
風
水

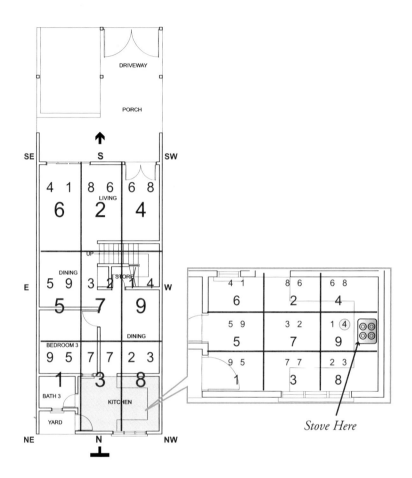

*Stove Here*

The kitchen, we have concluded in our basic analysis, is not ideal, being located in a palace with the #2-#3, a negative star combination known as Bullfight Sha which brings about arguments. Again, the Small Tai-Ji technique can be used to tackle the problem. Sub-divide the kitchen using the 9 Grids method, and then locate the stove or hob in the 1-4 combination location.

玄
空
飛
星
風
水

Bedroom 3 is already a good room as determined by the basic analysis. Using the Small Tai-Ji technique, we can also see that this bedroom has its door located at the 6-8 combination, which is a good door for the bedroom. For this room, locating the bed should be done carefully as the room is small and we don't want the Qi from the door to crash straight into the bed, creating an internal forms problem.

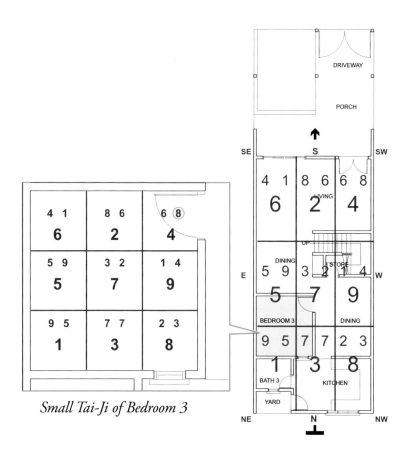

*Small Tai-Ji of Bedroom 3*

玄
空
飛
星
風
水

The staircase that leads upstairs is located at the West palace where there is a #1 and #4 Star. As the staircase is an active area of the house, the Facing Star is more likely to be activated, which is the #4 Star. This is a good star in general although not timely in Period 8 but is an acceptable star to have where the staircase is located. If we take a more advanced interpretation, the staircase is located at the 1-4 combination - this is a good combination, indicating scholastic success and academic achievement.

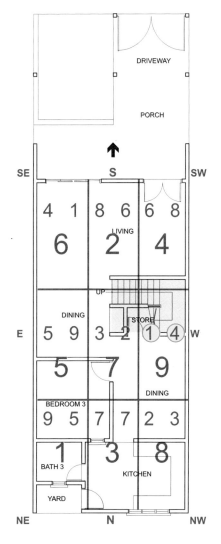

玄
空
飛
星
風
水

Moving on upstairs, we know the Master Bedroom is already in a good section of the house, but we want to know where to position the bed to maximise the Qi in this room for the occupants. The Small Tai-Ji technique can be used to determine the best location for the bed.

Assuming the owners are willing to place a screen in front of the door to deal with the small Forms problem, then we can safely have the bed located at the Sitting Star #8 palace, based on the Small Tai-Ji of the bedroom. In advanced Xuan Kong, placing the screen is also a good solution because the residents, in order to enter the bedroom, will by necessity have to walk into the Southwest palace, thus activating the #8 Facing Star.

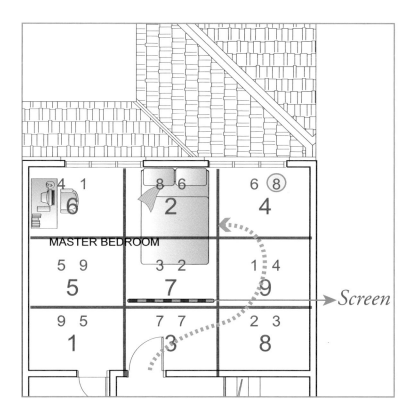

玄空飛星風水

Bedroom 2 is a good room, as we can see using the Small Tai-Ji technique. The room opens a 6-8 door and being bigger than Bedroom 3 downstairs, affords a little more luxury with the placement of the bed and the work desk. Sub-dividing the room using the 9 Grid method, the bed is best positioned at the back of the room, in the 9-5 palace, whilst the desk can be located at the 4-1 palace, near the front. The 1-4 palace is not so advisable for the desk as the Qi from the door comes right at the desk.

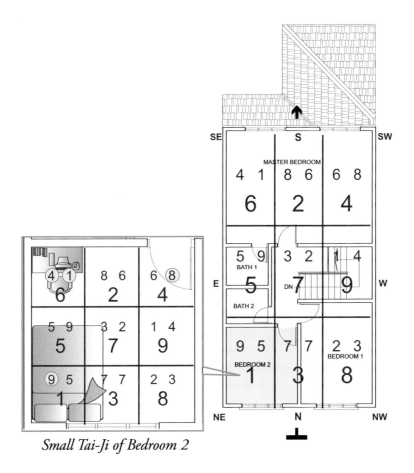

*Small Tai-Ji of Bedroom 2*

玄
空
飛
星
風
水

Bedroom 1 we have concluded should not be occupied because of the unfavourable stars located in this palace. However, using the Small Tai-Ji technique, this room can still be usable. Firstly, this room opens a 4-1 door – a great combination that denotes scholarly achievements, especially if it is occupied by a child. Secondly, the bed can be located right at the back, in the Northeast palace of the room, where the 9-5 is, to tap the #9 Sitting Star. Finally, the desk can be placed at the 1-4 location, which is again, conducive towards academic pursuits.

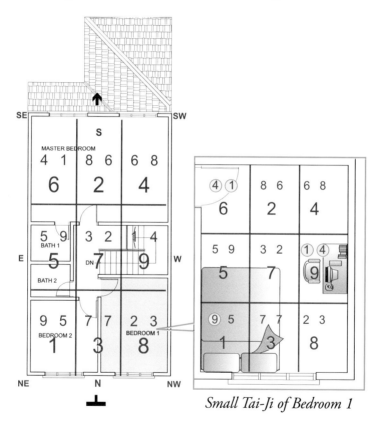

*Small Tai-Ji of Bedroom 1*

玄
空
飛
星
風
水

You may have noticed that there is a slight Forms problem – the door to the Master Bedroom is aligned with the door to Bedroom 2. Whilst this is a Forms issue, it is not a major problem – it is a relatively short distance between the two doors and so not significantly broad enough for the Qi to build up momentum and become serious Sha Qi.

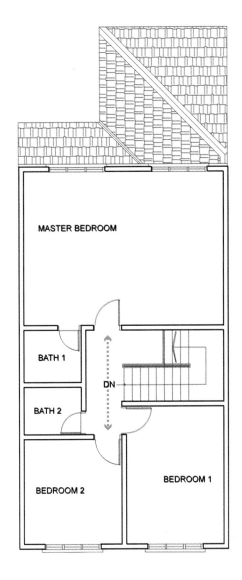

玄空飛星風水

In this example, we have not used a single cure in the form of an object or item placement and the solutions to the problems of the kitchen and Bedroom 1 we resolved through simply placing the bed and work desks in appropriate locations, to tap into the right stars, and using the rooms for the appropriate activity (Yin or Yang) to trigger the right stars. This is what Xuan Kong Flying Stars is really about!

Seemingly unusable rooms can also be rendered usable using advanced methods like combinations and the Small Tai-Ji method, although the importance of not using rooms with the #2, #3 and #5 stars still stands.

Xuan Kong Flying Stars Feng

玄空飛星風水

## Double Storey Bungalow House

The last property in our list of examples is a double storey bungalow house, completed in 2005. The owners would like to know if there is anything they can do to improve the Feng Shui of the property – they are already occupying the property. The property faces Northwest 1. Here is the Flying Star chart for a Northwest 1 Facing property in Period 8.

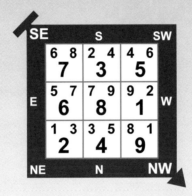

NW 1

Here is the floor plan of the double storey bungalow house.

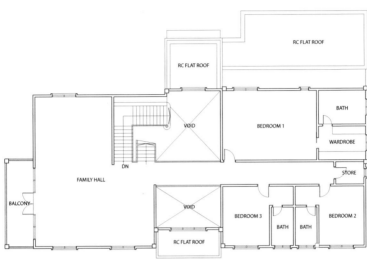

**1ST FLOOR PLAN**

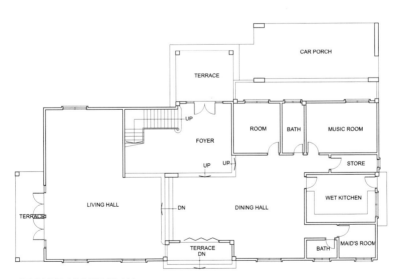

**GROUND FLOOR PLAN**

玄
空
飛
星
風
水

# Pre-Audit Preparation

As before, we do our homework before moving on to the analysis. Here, we also have an example of a property where the Main Door corresponds with the Facing of the property and also is roughly in the center of the facing façade, so you can stand at the Main Door to take the direction.

As this is a double storey house, you have to super-impose the Natal chart on BOTH the ground floor and the 1st floor of the house.

### Step 1: Divide the house using the 9 Grids

Remember, we don't include the open car porch in our 9 Grids as this is not a living area. Mark out the Palace directions for easy reference.

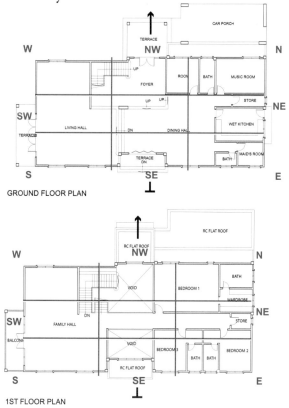

GROUND FLOOR PLAN

1ST FLOOR PLAN

玄空飛星風水

## Step 2: Super-impose the Natal Chart on the house floor plan

Transfer the Flying Stars from the Natal Chart into the house floor plan. Remember, transfer the Flying Stars to both the ground floor and the 1st floor plans. In contrast to the previous example, where the property is elongated horizontally this house is elongated vertically. We call this 'elongated Qi'. When a building is long, the Nine Palaces usually gets a bit cramped. It is more likely that rooms will overlap or span multiple palaces this way, resulting in mixed Qi. That is why we don't like elongated houses generally as the Qi is often mixed. If you are interested in understanding more about house shapes, you can refer to *Feng Shui for Homebuyers - Exteriors*.

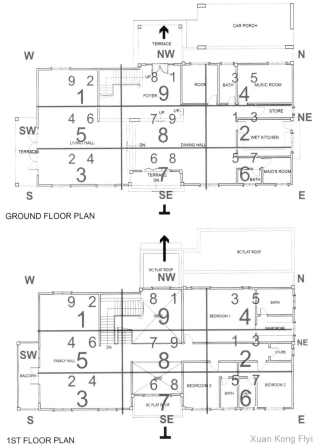

GROUND FLOOR PLAN

1ST FLOOR PLAN

玄
空
飛
星
風
水

# Feng Shui Analysis

## Basic Flying Stars Analysis

As always, we begin with the Main Door. This door opens where the #1 Facing Star is located, activating the #1 Facing Star. Since the #1 Star is one of the 3 timely stars in Period 8, this is a good door. It's not the best star to use of course because the #1 is the distant wealth star. But, a timely wealth star, even if the wealth is not immediate, is better than a negative star! So we can conclude this house has a reasonably good Main Door, although the occupants will probably have to look towards a more long-term business or look for long-term opportunities in wealth creation, or should expect their hard work to pay dividends only in the distant future.

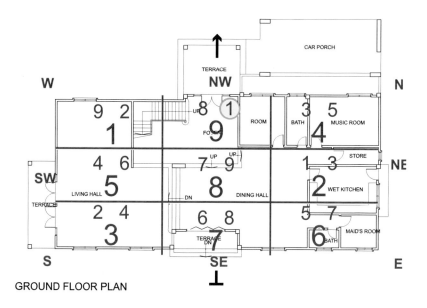

GROUND FLOOR PLAN

玄
空
飛
星
風
水

Now, I'm going to adjust the format of how we analyse this house a little bit. Let's take a look at where the negative stars are located. See the 3-5 lurking together in the music room in the North?

This is an example of where the 3-5 star combination is not something to be concerned about. The music room is probably a room used only periodically during the day or on occasion when there is a party at the property. So, we can say it is located in a suitable place because it is unlikely to be disturbed in the music room too often. So, nothing to sweat about!

*Ground Floor*

How about the kitchen? We have a kitchen in the Northeast palace, with a #1 Sitting Star and a #3 Facing Star. Now, although #3 is generally considered a bad star, elementally, #3 is a Wood star. As Wood produces Fire in the study of the Five Elements, so #3 can be used for the kitchen. Of course, preferably we should have the kitchen located in a palace with positive and timely stars. But in a push, the #3, like the #4, is usable because elementally, it is in line with the use of fire in the kitchen for cooking (and this is applicable irrespective of whether you use electric or real fire.) This property's kitchen therefore passes the test.

玄
空
飛
星
風
水

The bedrooms in this property are a little trickier. The Master Bedroom is located where the #3 and #5 both reside. Automatically, this makes the Master Bedroom unusable. The fix is of course not hard – there is a large area of space set aside for the family room so part of this space can be turned into the Master Bedroom. Preferably of course, we want to use the Sitting Star #9, so the West palace is the best place to locate the bedroom. This does mean the entire space set aside for the Master Bedroom at present is not usable.

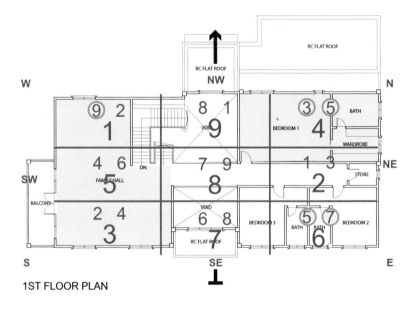

1ST FLOOR PLAN

Bedrooms 2 and 3 are also not located in a particularly good part of the house. Neither the #5 Sitting Star or the #7 Facing Star are usable or suitable for use in a bedroom.

Now, you may have noticed that because of the way the stars fly, a good 1/3 of this house has no usable rooms, especially upstairs. Accordingly, the owner may have to consider some significant renovations, in order to be able to better utilise the favourable sections of the house.

玄
空
飛
星
風
水

One redeeming point is the location of the rear terrace door on the ground floor. Here the door is located at palace where the #8 Facing Star resides. As it is unlikely that the owners will be using the terrace door too much, it is probably a good idea to place a water feature here, and if possible, have a fish pond outside the back, to activate the #8 Facing Star. This, coupled with the #1 Facing Star at the Main Door, will mean 2 out of 3 of the timely stars in Period 8 are being activated in this property.

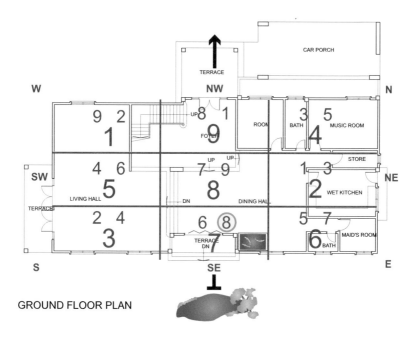

**GROUND FLOOR PLAN**

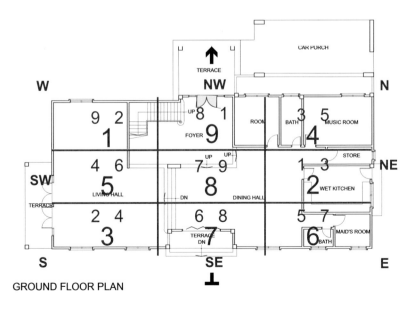

**8** Practical Application of Xuan Kong Flying Stars

玄空飛星風水

# Advanced Flying Stars analysis

Now, basic Flying Stars analysis tells us this property has a good Main Door. At the more advanced level, when we consider the Direct-Indirect Spirit principle, this door is not so favourable. This is because the Northwest is the Direct Spirit location and we want things to be Yin or still in the Direct Spirit location.

This is a case where the basic analysis ties in with the advanced analysis and arrives at the same conclusion. Sure, the door is NOT THAT GOOD – both on the advanced analysis and the basic analysis. But it is not bad either. Non-conformity to the Direct-Indirect Spirit principle means making money is a little bit more uphill for the residents of this property – it comes a lot slower. But as it is, the door is using the #1 Facing Star, which is the star of future wealth. So it's going to be slow-going anyway.

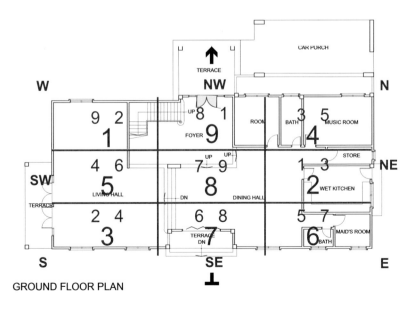

GROUND FLOOR PLAN

玄空飛星風水

I would deploy the Small Tai-Ji technique to help determine the location of the kitchen stove here, and locate the stove at the 1-3 location.

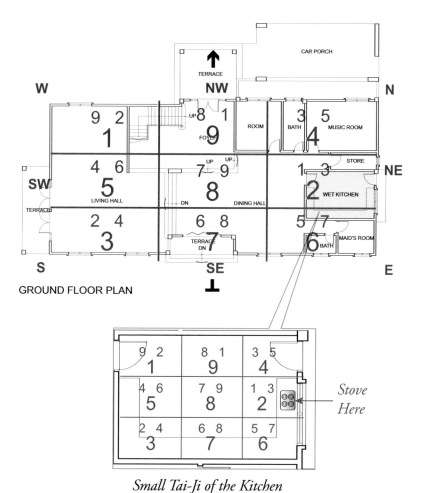

*Small Tai-Ji of the Kitchen*

玄空飛星風水

Earlier it was suggested that a water feature or aquarium be placed at the 6-8 location to help activate the #8 Facing Star. I would further recommend the owners build a bar at the foyer area to solve the small Internal Forms problem. Notice how the Main Door is in a straight line with the sliding door exit to the back terrace? This is a negative internal form, and as I explained in *Feng Shui for Homebuyers - Interiors* we don't like the Main Door to open to another door. The Qi then has no chance to collect inside the property and circulate. It rushes straight through the house.

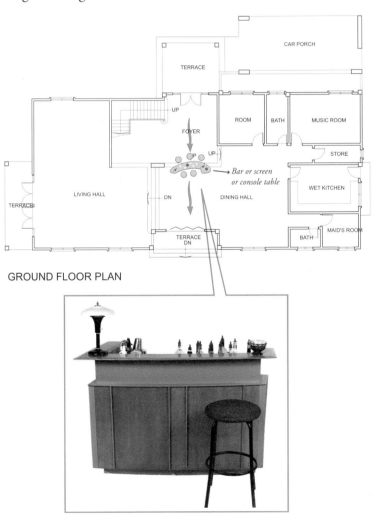

GROUND FLOOR PLAN

玄
空
飛
星
風
水

The Small Tai-Ji technique can also help with the problematic bedrooms upstairs. I would continue to recommend avoiding the use of the 3-5 room for the Master Bedroom. However, if pressed, using the Small Tai-Ji technique, and if the bedroom door is moved, the room could be made usable. The owners would have to renovate, move the door to the 6-8 location, and place their bed at the 9-2. However in general, the presence of the #3 and #5 together means the room is already unusable. We prefer to use the Small Tai-Ji technique for refining a room that is already good or refining a room that is average, to make it a little better. It is generally not a good idea to use this technique to make a bad room a little bit more usable!

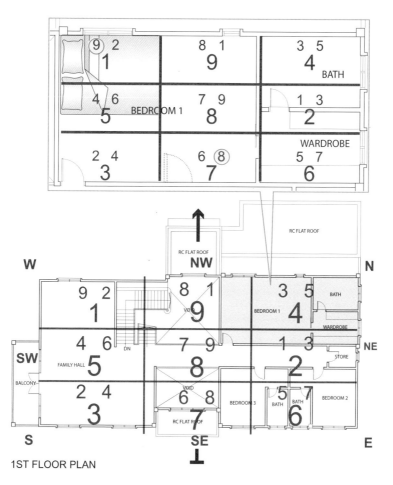

玄空飛星風水

What if the owners are willing to renovate the family hall area to turn that into a Master Bedroom? Based on the Small Tai-Ji technique, they will have to endure some space wastage, and reduce the size of the Master Bedroom in order to open a good door. This is because the bedroom door should not open at the 4-3 or 5-7 location. The 4-3 combination indicates challenges, work and professional rivalry and persistent bickering. The 5-7 combination frequently brings about food poisoning, gastro-intestinal ailments or arguments. But opening the door at the bottom of the marked area, they will have their bedroom door at the 6-8 location. The bed can then be placed at the 9-2 in the corner as the Sitting Star #9 is suitable for the bed location.

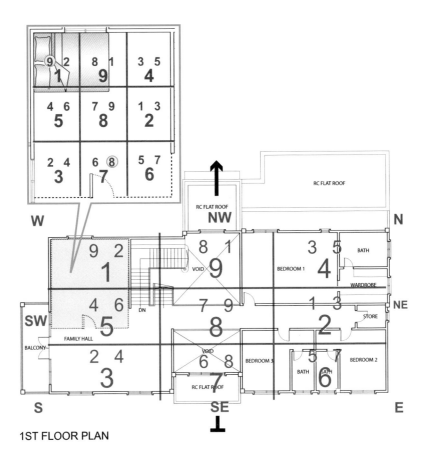

**1ST FLOOR PLAN**

玄
空
飛
星
風
水

Bedroom 2 and 3, although located in a palace with not-so-favourable stars (the #5 and #7), are not that bad when we look at things from the Small Tai-Ji technique perspective. Both the rooms open 8-1 doors, which is a good location for the bedroom door. The bed can easily be located at the 9-2, with the study desk at the 6-8 location, near the bottom of both rooms.

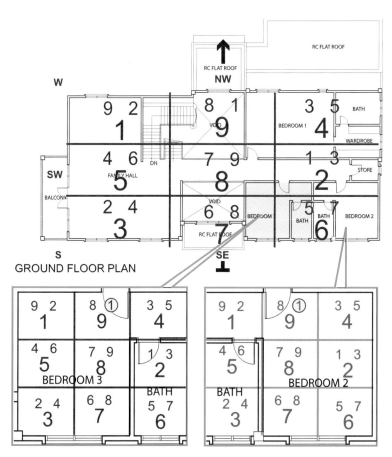

GROUND FLOOR PLAN

Of course, there could be a small forms problem especially with bedroom 3 because the room is small and quite tight and the desk must be positioned in a manner that the Qi does not crash at the back of the person sitting at the desk. Bedroom 3 also makes it a little bit hard to position the bed because of the small space between the bathroom and the door. So it might be an idea, if the owners plan to renovate, to move the bathroom to the right side of bedroom 3.

玄
空
飛
星
風
水

## Beyond Flying Stars

Xuan Kong Flying Stars is of course only a small sub-system in the Xuan Kong system of Feng Shui. And Xuan Kong itself is but a part of the larger San Yuan system. So there's much, much more to learn if you are interested in Feng Shui.

And for those of you seeking simply to understand simple Flying Stars, you would have by this stage learnt enough Flying Stars to be able to audit your own house, and effect some simple solutions to the typical problems. But to truly make use of Flying Stars, it is essential to have knowledge of the Combinations and also to be able to recognise special structures like the Pearl String, Parent String or Combination of Ten structures, and to learn to make use of special formations like the Castle Gate Theory and 7 Star Robbery. Then there is the divination aspect of Xuan Kong which is a very powerful component of Xuan Kong Flying Stars.

In my next book for the *Xuan Kong Feng Shui* series, I will show you how to use Combinations effectively to unlock the full potential of your property, and make use of the annual changing Qi, in the form of the annual star. Till then, have a go at auditing your own house (or maybe even your friend's house) and have fun with Flying Stars.

# About Joey Yap

**Joey Yap** is the Founder and Master Trainer of the Mastery Academy of Chinese Metaphysics, a global organisation devoted to the worldwide teaching of Feng Shui, BaZi, Mian Xiang, Yi Jing and other Chinese Metaphysics subjects. Joey is also the Founder of Yap Global Consulting, an international Feng Shui and Chinese Astrology consulting firm offering audit and consultation services to corporations and individuals all over the world.

Joey received his formal education in Malaysia and Australia. He has combined the best of Eastern learning and Western education systems in the teaching methodology practiced at the Academy. Students of the Mastery Academy study traditional syllabuses of Chinese Metaphysics but through Western-style modular programs that are structured and systematic, enabling individuals to easily and quickly learn, grasp and master complex Chinese Metaphysics subjects like Feng Shui and BaZi. These unique structured learning systems are also utilized by Mastery Academy instructors all over the world to teach BaZi and Feng Shui.

The Mastery Academy is also the first international educational organisation to fully utilize the benefits of the Internet to promote continuous education, encourage peer-to-peer learning, enable mentoring and distance learning. Students interact with each other live, and continue to learn and improve their knowledge.

Despite his busy schedule, Joey continues to write for the Mastery Journal, a monthly eZine on Feng Shui and Astrology devoted for world-wide readers and the production of the world's first bilingual *Ten Thousand Year Calendar*. He is also the best selling author of *Stories and Lessons on Feng Shui, Mian Xiang- Discover Face Reading, Tong Shu Diary, BaZi - The Destiny Code, BaZi - The Destiny Code Revealed, Feng Shui for Homebuyers-Interior, Feng Shui for Homebuyers-Exterior* and the *Mini Feng Shui Compass*. Besides being a regular guest of various radio and TV talk shows, Joey is also a regular columnist for a national newspaper and various magazines in Malaysia. In fact, he hosted his own *TV series, Discover Feng Shui with Joey Yap*, on Malaysia's 8TV channel in 2005; a popular program that focused on heightening awareness of Feng Shui and Chinese Metaphysics.

A firm believer in innovation being the way forward, Joey recently released the BaZi Ming Pan 2.0 software, which allows users to generate configurable, detailed BaZi charts.

Author's personal website: www.joeyyap.com
Academy website: www.masteryacademy.com | www.masteryjournal.com
| www.maelearning.com

# EDUCATION
## The Mastery Academy of Chinese Metaphysics:
## the first choice for practitioners and aspiring students of the
## art and science of Chinese Classical Feng Shui and Astrology.

For thousands of years, Eastern knowledge has been passed from one generation to another through the system of discipleship. A venerated master would accept suitable individuals at a young age as his disciples, and informally through the years, pass on his knowledge and skills to them. His disciples in turn, would take on their own disciples, as a means to perpetuate knowledge or skills.

This system served the purpose of restricting the transfer of knowledge to only worthy honourable individuals and ensuring that outsiders or Westerners would not have access to thousands of years of Eastern knowledge, learning and research.

However, the disciple system has also resulted in Chinese Metaphysics and Classical Studies lacking systematic teaching methods. Knowledge garnered over the years has not been accumulated in a concise, systematic manner, but scattered amongst practitioners, each practicing his/her knowledge, art and science, in isolation.

The disciple system, out of place in today's modern world, endangers the advancement of these classical fields that continue to have great relevance and application today.

At the Mastery Academy of Chinese Metaphysics, our Mission is to bring Eastern Classical knowledge in the fields of metaphysics, Feng Shui and Astrology sciences and the arts to the world. These Classical teachings and knowledge, previously shrouded in secrecy and passed on only through the discipleship system, are adapted into structured learning, which can easily be understood, learnt and mastered. Through modern learning methods, these renowned ancient arts, sciences and practices can be perpetuated while facilitating more extensive application and understanding of these classical subjects.

The Mastery Academy espouses an educational philosophy that draws from the best of the East and West . It is the world's premier educational institution for the study of Chinese Metaphysics Studies offering a wide range and variety of courses, ensuring that students have the opportunity to pursue their preferred field of study and enabling existing practitioners and professionals to gain cross-disciplinary knowledge that complements their current field of practice.

Courses at the Mastery Academy have been carefully designed to ensure a comprehensive yet compact syllabus. The modular nature of the courses enables students to immediately begin to put their knowledge into practice while pursuing continued study of their field and complementary fields. Students thus have the benefit of developing and gaining practical experience in tandem with the expansion and advancement of their theoretical knowledge.

Students can also choose from a variety of study options, from a distance learning program, the Homestudy Series, that enables study at one's own pace or intensive foundation courses and compact lecture-based courses, held in various cities around the world by Joey Yap or our licensed instructors. The Mastery Academy's faculty and make-up is international in nature, thus ensuring that prospective students can attend courses at destinations nearest to their country of origin or with a licensed Mastery Academy instructor in their home country.

The Mastery Academy provides 24x7 support to students through its Online Community, with a variety of tools, documents, forums and e-learning materials to help students stay at the forefront of research in their fields and gain invaluable assistance from peers and mentoring from their instructors.

™

# MASTERY ACADEMY
## OF CHINESE METAPHYSICS

### www.masteryacademy.com

**MALAYSIA**
19-3, The Boulevard
Mid Valley City
59200 Kuala Lumpur, Malaysia
Tel    : +603-2284 8080
Fax   : +603-2284 1218
Email : info@masteryacademy.com

**SINGAPORE**
14, Robinson Road # 13-00
Far East Finance Building
Singapore 048545
Tel    : +65-6722 8775
Fax   : +65-3125 7131
Email  : singapore@masteryacademy.com

**AUSTRALIA**
PO Box 692,
Bentley WA 6982, Australia
Tel    : +618-9262 0468
Fax   : +618-9262 0469
Email : australia@masteryacademy.com

Represented in:
Australia, Austria, Brazil, Canada, China, Cyprus, France, Germany, Greece, Hungary, India, Japan, Indonesia, Italy, Malaysia, Mexico, Netherlands, New Zealand, Philippines, Russian Federation, Poland, Singapore, South Africa, Switzerland, Turkey, U.S.A., Ukraine, United Kingdom

# Introducing...
## The Mastery Academy's E-Learning Center!

The Mastery Academy's goal has always been to share authentic knowledge of Chinese Metaphysics with the whole world.

Nevertheless, we do recognize that distance, time, and hotel and traveling costs – amongst many other factors – could actually hinder people from enrolling for a classroom-based course. But with the advent and amazing advance of IT today, NOT any more!

With this in mind, we have invested heavily in IT, to conceive what is probably the first and only E-Learning Center in the world today that offers a full range of studies in the field of Chinese Metaphysics.

Convenient          Study from Your          Easy Enrollment
                     Own Home

## The Mastery Academy's E-Learning Center

Now, armed with your trusty computer or laptop, and Internet access, knowledge of classical Feng Shui, BaZi (Destiny Analysis) and Mian Xiang (Face Reading) are but a literal click away!

Study at your own pace, and interact with your Instructor and fellow students worldwide, from anywhere in the world. With our E-Learning Center, knowledge of Chinese Metaphysics is brought DIRECTLY to you in all its clarity – topic-by-topic, and lesson-by-lesson; with illustrated presentations and comprehensive notes expediting your learning curve!

Your education journey through our E-Learning Center may be done via any of the following approaches:

## 1. Online Courses

There are 3 Programs available: our Online Feng Shui Program, Online BaZi Program, and Online Mian Xiang Program. Each Program consists of several Levels, with each Level consisting of many Lessons in turn. Each Lesson contains a pre-recorded video session on the topic at hand, accompanied by presentation-slides and graphics as well as downloadable tutorial notes that you can print and file for future reference.

Video Lecture    Presentation    Downloadable
        Slide      Notes

## 2. MA Live!

MA Live!, as its name implies, enables LIVE broadcasts of Joey Yap's courses and seminars – right to your computer screen. Students will not only get to see and hear Joey talk on real-time 'live', but also participate and more importantly, TALK to Joey via the MA Live! interface. All the benefits of a live class, minus the hassle of actually having to attend one!

**How It Works**

Our Live Classes     You at Home

## 3. Video-On-Demand (VOD)

Get immediate streaming-downloads of the Mastery Academy's wide range of educational DVDs, right on your computer screen. No more shipping costs and waiting time to be incurred!

**Instant VOD Online**

Choose From Our list    Click "Play" on Your PC
of Available VODs!

Welcome to **www.maelearning.com**; the web portal of our E-Learning Center, and YOUR virtual gateway to Chinese Metaphysics!

# Mastery Academy around the world

Canada

United States

Mexico

Brazil

United Kingdom

France
Netherlands
Switzerland
Italy
Cyprus

Germany
Austria
Poland

Greece
Hungary

Turkey

Russian
Federation

Ukraine

China

Japan

India

South Africa

Philippines
Kuala Lumpur
Malaysia

Indonesia

Singapore

Australia

New Zealand

# YAP GLOBAL CONSULTING

## Joey Yap & Yap Global Consulting

Headed by Joey Yap, Yap Global Consulting (YGC) is a leading international consulting firm specializing in Feng Shui, Mian Xiang (Face Reading) and BaZi (Destiny Analysis) consulting services worldwide. Joey - an internationally renowned Master Trainer, Consultant, Speaker and best-selling Author - has dedicated his life to the art and science of Chinese Metaphysics.

YGC has its main offices in Kuala Lumpur and Australia, and draws upon its diverse reservoir of strength from a group of dedicated and experienced consultants based in more than 30 countries, worldwide.

As the pioneer in blending established, classical Chinese Metaphysics techniques with the latest approach in consultation practices, YGC has built its reputation on the principles of professionalism and only the highest standards of service. This allows us to retain the cutting edge in delivering Feng Shui and Destiny consultation services to both corporate and personal clients, in a simple and direct manner, without compromising on quality.

## Across Industries: Our Portfolio of Clients

Our diverse portfolio of both corporate and individual clients from all around the world bears testimony to our experience and capabilities.

Virtually every industry imaginable has benefited from our services - ranging from academic and financial institutions, real-estate developers and multinational corporations, to those in the leisure and tourism industry. Our services are also engaged by professionals, prominent business personalities, celebrities, high-profile politicians and people from all walks of life.

---

## YAP GLOBAL GONSULTING

Name (Mr./Mrs./Ms.): _____

Contact Details _____

Tel: _____ Fax: _____

Mobile : _____

E-mail: _____

**What Type of Consultation Are You Interested In?**
☐ Feng Shui   ☐ BaZi   ☐ Date Selection   ☐ Yi Jing

**Please tick if applicable:**
☐ Are you a Property Developer looking to engage Yap Global Consulting?

☐ Are you a Property Investor looking for tailor-made packages to suit your investment requirements?

**Please attach your name card here.**

**Thank you for completing this form.**
Please fax it back to us at:

| Singapore | Australia | Malaysia & the rest of the world |
|---|---|---|
| Fax: +65-3125 7131 | Fax: +618-9262 0469 | Fax: +603-2284 2213 |
| Tel : +65-6722 8775 | Tel : +618-9262 0468 | Tel : +603-2284 1213 |

# Feng Shui Consultations

## For Residential Properties
- Initial Land/Property Assessment
- Residential Feng Shui Consultations
- Residential Land Selection
- End-to-End Residential Consultation

## For Commercial Properties
- Initial Land/Property Assessment
- Commercial Feng Shui Consultations
- Commercial Land Selection
- End-to-End Commercial Consultation

## For Property Developers
- End-to-End Consultation
- Post-Consultation Advisory Services
- Panel Feng Shui Consultant

## For Property Investors
- Your Personal Feng Shui Consultant
- Tailor-Made Packages

## For Memorial Parks & Burial Sites
- Yin House Feng Shui

# BaZi Consultations

## Personal Destiny Analysis
- Personal Destiny Analysis for Individuals
- Children's BaZi Analysis
- Family BaZi Analysis

## Strategic Analysis for Corporate Organizations
- Corporate BaZi Consultations
- BaZi Analysis for Human Resource Management

## Entrepreneurs & Business Owners
- BaZi Analysis for Entrepreneurs

## Career Pursuits
- BaZi Career Analysis

## Relationships
- Marriage and Compatibility Analysis
- Partnership Analysis

## For Everyone
- Annual BaZi Forecast
- Your Personal BaZi Coach

# Date Selection Consultations

- **Marriage Date Selection**
- **Caesarean Birth Date Selection**
- **House-Moving Date Selection**
- **Renovation & Groundbreaking Dates**

- **Signing of Contracts**
- **Official Openings**
- **Product Launches**

# Yi Jing Assessment

## A Time-Tested, Accurate Science

- With a history predating 4 millennia, the Yi Jing - or Classic of Change - is one of the oldest Chinese texts surviving today. Its purpose as an oracle, in predicting the outcome of things, is based on the variables of Time, Space and Specific Events.

- A Yi Jing Assessment provides specific answers to any specific questions you may have about a specific event or endeavor. This is something that a Destiny Analysis would not be able to give you.

Basically, what a Yi Jing Assessment does is focus on only ONE aspect or item at a particular point in your life, and give you a calculated prediction of the details that will follow suit, if you undertake a particular action. It gives you an insight into a situation, and what course of action to take in order to arrive at a satisfactory outcome at the end of the day.

Please Contact YGC for a personalized Yi Jing Assessment!

# INVITING US TO YOUR CORPORATE EVENTS

Many reputable organizations and institutions have worked closely with YGC to build a synergistic business relationship by engaging our team of consultants, led by Joey Yap, as speakers at their corporate events. Our seminars and short talks are always packed with audiences consisting of clients and associates of multinational and public-listed companies as well as key stakeholders of financial institutions.

We tailor our seminars and talks to suit the anticipated or pertinent group of audience. Be it a department, subsidiary, your clients or even the entire corporation, we aim to fit your requirements in delivering the intended message(s).

# Latest DVDs Release by Joey Yap
# Feng Shui for Homebuyers DVD Series

Best-selling Author, and international Master Trainer and Consultant Joey Yap reveals in these DVDs the significant Feng Shui features that every homebuyer should know when evaluating a property.

Joey will guide you on how to customise your home to maximise the Feng Shui potential of your property and gain the full benefit of improving your health, wealth and love life using the 9 Palace Grid. He will show you how to go about applying the classical applications of the Life Gua and House Gua techniques to get attuned to your Sheng Qi (positive energies).

In these DVDs, you will also learn how to identify properties with good Feng Shui features that will help you promote a fulfilling life and achieve your full potential. Discover how to avoid properties with negative Feng Shui that can bring about detrimental effects to your health, wealth and relationships.

Joey will also elaborate on how to fix the various aspects of your home that may have an impact on the Feng Shui of your property and give pointers on how to tap into the positive energies to support your goals.

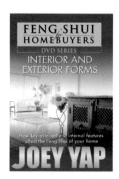

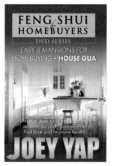

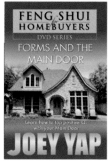

# Feng Shui for Homebuyers Series

### Feng Shui For Homebuyers - Exterior

Best selling Author and international Feng Shui Consultant, Joey Yap, will guide you on the various important features in your external environment that have a bearing on the Feng Shui of your home. For homeowners, those looking to build their own home or even investors who are looking to apply Feng Shui to their homes, this book provides valuable information from the classical Feng Shui theories and applications.

This book will assist you in screening and eliminating unsuitable options with negative FSQ (Feng Shui Quotient) should you acquire your own land or if you are purchasing a newly built home. It will also help you in determining which plot of land to select and which to avoid when purchasing an empty parcel of land.

### Feng Shui for Homebuyers - Interior

A book every homeowner or potential house buyer should have. The Feng Shui for Homebuyers (Interior) is an informative reference book and invaluable guide written by best selling Author and international Feng Shui Consultant, Joey Yap.

This book provides answers to the important questions of what really does matter when looking at the internal Feng Shui of a home or office. It teaches you how to analyze your home or office floor plans and how to improve their Feng Shui. It will answer all your questions about the positive and negative flow of Qi within your home and ways to utilize them to your maximum benefit.

Providing you with a guide to calculating your Life Gua and House Gua to fine-tune your Feng Shui within your property, Joey Yap focuses on practical, easily applicable ideas on what you can implement internally in a property.

# Discover Feng Shui with Joey Yap (TV Series)

### Discover Feng Shui with Joey Yap: Set of 4 DVDs

**Informative and entertaining, classical Feng Shui comes alive in *Discover Feng Shui with Joey Yap!***

Dying to know how you can use Feng Shui to improve your house or office, but simply too busy attend for formal classes?

You have the questions. Now let Joey personally answer them in this 4-set DVD compilation! Learn how to ensure the viability of your residence or workplace, Feng Shui-wise, without having to convert it into a Chinese antiques' shop. Classical Feng Shui is about harnessing the natural power of your environment to improve quality of life. It's a systematic and subtle metaphysical science.

And that's not all. Joey also debunks many a myth about classical Feng Shui, and shares with viewers Face Reading tips as well!

Own the series that national channel 8TV did a re-run of in 2005, today!

# Educational Tools & Software

## Mini Feng Shui Compass

This Mini Feng Shui Compass with the accompanying Companion Booklet written by leading Feng Shui and Chinese Astrology Master Trainer Joey Yap is a must-have for any Feng Shui enthusiast.

The Mini Feng Shui Compass is a self-aligning compass that is not only light at 100gms but also built sturdily to ensure it will be convenient to use anywhere. The rings on the Mini Feng Shui Compass are bi-lingual and incorporate the 24 Mountain Rings that is used in your traditional Luo Pan.

The comprehensive booklet included will guide you in applying the 24 Mountain Directions on your Mini Feng Shui Compass effectively and the 8 Mansions Feng Shui to locate the most auspicious locations within your home, office and surroundings. You can also use the Mini Feng Shui Compass when measuring the direction of your property for the purpose of applying Flying Stars Feng Shui.

## BaZi Ming Pan Software Version 2.0
Professional Four Pillars Calculator for Destiny Analysis

The BaZi Ming Pan Version 2.0 Professional Four Pillars Calculator for Destiny Analysis is the most technically advanced software of its kind in the world today. It allows even those without any knowledge of BaZi to generate their own BaZi Charts, and provides virtually every detail required to undertake a comprehensive Destiny Analysis.

This Professional Four Pillars Calculator allows you to even undertake a day-to-day analysis of your Destiny. What's more, all BaZi Charts generated by this software are fully printable and configurable! Designed for both enthusiasts and professional practitioners, this state-of-the-art software blends details with simplicity, and is capable of generating 4 different types of BaZi charts: **BaZi Professional Charts, BaZi Annual Analysis Charts, BaZi Pillar Analysis Charts and BaZi Family Relationship Charts.**

Additional references, configurable to cater to all levels of BaZi knowledge and usage, include:
• Dual Age & Bilingual Option (Western & Chinese) • Na Yin narrations • 12 Life Stages evaluation • Death & Emptiness • Gods & Killings • Special Days • Heavenly Virtue Nobles

This software also comes with a Client Management feature that allows you to save and trace clients' records instantly, navigate effortlessly between BaZi charts, and file your clients' information in an organized manner.

The BaZi Ming Pan Version 2.0 Calculator sets a new standard by combining the best of BaZi and technology.

# Accelerate Your Face Reading Skills With
# Joey Yap's Face Reading Revealed DVD Series

Mian Xiang, the Chinese art of Face Reading, is an ancient form of physiognomy and entails the use of the face and facial characteristics to evaluate key aspects of a person's life, luck and destiny. In his Face Reading DVDs series, Joey Yap shows you how the facial features reveal a wealth of information about a person's luck, destiny and personality.

Mian Xiang also tell us the talents, quirks and personality of an individual. Do you know that just by looking at a person's face, you can ascertain his or her health, wealth, relationships and career? Let Joey Yap show you how the 12 Palaces can be utilised to reveal a person's inner talents, characteristics and much more.

Each facial feature on the face represents one year in a person's life. Your face is a 100-year map of your life and each position reveals your fortune and destiny at a particular age as well as insights and information about your personality, skills, abilities and destiny.

Using Mian Xiang, you will also be able to plan your life ahead by identifying, for example, the right business partner and knowing the sort of person that you need to avoid. By knowing their characteristics through the facial features, you will be able to gauge their intentions and gain an upper hand in negotiations.

Do you know what moles signify? Do they bring good or bad luck? Do you want to build better relationships with your partner or family members or have your ever wondered why you seem to be always bogged down by trivial problems in your life?

In these highly entertaining DVDs, Joey will help you answer all these questions and more. You will be able to ascertain the underlying meaning of moles, birthmarks or even the type of your hair in Face Reading. Joey will also reveal the guidelines to help you foster better and stronger relationships with your loved ones through Mian Xiang.

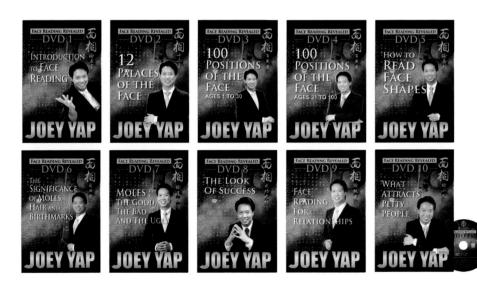

# Continue Your Journey with Joey Yap's Books

## BaZi - The Destiny Code (English & Chinese versions)

Leading Chinese Astrology Master Trainer Joey Yap makes it easy to learn how to unlock your Destiny through your BaZi with this book. BaZi or Four Pillars of Destiny is an ancient Chinese science which enables individuals to understand their personality, hidden talents and abilities as well as their luck cycle, simply by examining the information contained within their birth data. The Destiny Code is the first book that shows readers how to plot and interpret their own Destiny Charts and lays the foundation for more in-depth BaZi studies. Written in a lively entertaining style, the Destiny Code makes BaZi accessible to the layperson. Within 10 chapters, understand and appreciate more about this astoundingly accurate ancient Chinese Metaphysical science.

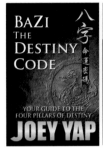

## BaZi - The Destiny Code Revealed

In this follow up to Joey Yap's best-selling The Destiny Code, delve deeper into your own Destiny chart through an understanding of the key elemental relationships that affect the Heavenly Stems and Earthly Branches. Find out how Combinations, Clash, Harm, Destructions and Punishments bring new dimension to a BaZi chart. Complemented by extensive real-life examples, The Destiny Code Revealed takes you to the next level of BaZi, showing you how to unlock the Codes of Destiny and to take decisive action at the right time, and capitalise on the opportunities in life.

## The Ten Thousand Year Calendar

The Ten Thousand Year Calendar or 萬年曆 Wan Nian Li is a regular reference book and an invaluable tool used by masters, practitioners and students of Feng Shui, BaZi (Four Pillars of Destiny), Chinese Zi Wei Dou Shu Astrology (Purple Star), Yi Jing (I-Ching) and Date Selection specialists.

JOEY YAP's Ten Thousand Year Calendar provides the Gregorian (Western) dates converted into both the Chinese Solar and Lunar calendar in both the English and Chinese language.

It also includes a comprehensive set of key Feng Shui and Chinese Astrology charts and references, including Xuan Kong Nine Palace Flying Star Charts, Monthly and Daily Flying Stars, Water Dragon Formulas Reference Charts, Zi Wei Dou Shu (Purple Star) Astrology Reference Charts, BaZi (Four Pillars of Destiny) Heavenly Stems, Earthly Branches and all other related reference tables for Chinese Metaphysical Studies.

# Annual Releases

## Chinese Astrology for 2008

This information-packed annual guide to the Chinese Astrology for 2008 goes way beyond the conventional `animal horoscope' book. To begin with, author Joey Yap includes a personalized outlook for 2008 based on the individual's BaZi Day Pillar (Jia Zi) and a 12-month micro-analysis for each of the 60 Day Pillars – in addition to the annual outlook for all 12 animal signs and the 12-month outlook for each animal sign in 2008. Find out what awaits you in 2008 from the four key aspects of Health, Wealth, Career and Relationships... with Joey Yap's **Chinese Astrology for 2008**!

## Feng Shui for 2008

Maximize the Qi of the Year of the Earth Rat for your home and office, with Joey Yap's **Feng Shui for 2008** book. Learn how to tap into the positive sectors of the year, and avoid the negative ones and those with the Annual Afflictions, as well as ascertain how the annual Flying Stars affect your property by comparing them against the Eight Mansions (Ba Zhai) for 2008. Flying Stars enthusiasts will also find this book handy, as it includes the monthly Flying Stars charts for the year, accompanied by detailed commentaries on what sectors to use and avoid – to enable you to optimize your Academic, Relationships and Wealth Luck in 2008.

## Tong Shu Diary 2008

Organize your professional and personal lives with the **Tong Shu Diary 2008**, with a twist... it also allows you to determine the most suitable dates on which you can undertake important activities and endeavors throughout the year! This compact Diary integrates the Chinese Solar and Lunar Calendars with the universal lingua franca of the Gregorian Calendar.

## Tong Shu Monthly Planner 2008

Tailor-made for the Feng Shui or BaZi enthusiast in you, or even professional Chinese Metaphysics consultants who want a compact planner with useful information incorporated into it. In the **Tong Shu Monthly Planner 2008**, you will find the auspicious and inauspicious dates for the year marked out for you, alongside the most suitable activities to be undertaken on each day. As a bonus, there is also a reference section containing all the monthly Flying Stars charts and Annual Afflictions for 2008.

## Tong Shu Desktop Calendar 2008

Get an instant snapshot of the suitable and unsuitable activities for each day of the Year of the Earth Rat, with the icons displayed on this lightweight Desktop Calendar. Elegantly presenting the details of the Chinese Solar Calendar in the form of the standard Gregorian one, the **Tong Shu Desktop Calendar 2008** is perfect for Chinese Metaphysics enthusiasts and practitioners alike. Whether it a business launching or meeting, ground breaking ceremony, travel or house-moving that you have in mind, this Calendar is designed to fulfill your information needs.

## Tong Shu Year Planner 2008

This one-piece Planner presents you all the essential information you need for significant activities or endeavors...with just a quick glance! In a nutshell, it allows you to identify the favorable and unfavorable days, which will in turn enable you to schedule your year's activities so as to make the most of good days, and avoid the ill-effects brought about by inauspicious ones.

# Continue Your Journey with Joey Yap's Books

## Mian Xiang - Discover Face Reading

Need to identify a suitable business partner? How about understanding your staff or superiors better? Or even choosing a suitable spouse? These mind boggling questions can be answered in Joey Yap's introductory book to Face Reading titled *Mian Xiang – Discover Face Reading*. This book will help you discover the hidden secrets in a person's face.

*Mian Xiang – Discover Face Reading* is comprehensive book on all areas of Face Reading, covering some of the most important facial features, including the forehead, mouth, ears and even the philtrum above your lips. This book will help you analyse not just your Destiny but help you achieve your full potential and achieve life fulfillment.

## Stories and Lessons on Feng Shui (English & Chinese versions)

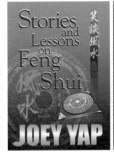 

*Stories and Lessons on Feng Shui* is a compilation of essays and stories written by leading Feng Shui and Chinese Astrology trainer and consultant Joey Yap about Feng Shui and Chinese Astrology.

In this heart-warming collection of easy to read stories, find out why it's a myth that you should never have Water on the right hand side of your house, the truth behind the infamous 'love' and 'wealth' corners and that the sudden death of a pet fish is really NOT due to bad luck!

## More Stories and Lessons on Feng Shui

Finally, the long-awaited sequel to *Stories & Lessons on Feng Shui*!

If you've read the best-selling Stories & Lessons on Feng Shui, you won't want to miss this book. And even if you haven't read *Stories & Lessons on Feng Shui*, there's always a time to rev your Feng Shui engine up.

The time is NOW.

And the book? *More Stories & Lessons on Feng Shui* – the 2nd compilation of the most popular articles and columns penned by Joey Yap; **specially featured in national and international publications, magazines and newspapers.**

All in all, *More Stories & Lessons on Feng Shui* is a delightful chronicle of Joey's articles, thoughts and vast experience - as a professional Feng Shui consultant and instructor - that have been purposely refined, edited and expanded upon to make for a light-hearted, interesting yet educational read. And with Feng Shui, BaZi, Mian Xiang and Yi Jing all thrown into this one dish, there's something for everyone...so all you need to serve or accompany *More Stories & Lessons on Feng Shui* with is your favorite cup of tea or coffee!

# Continue Your Journey with Joey Yap's Books

## Xuan Kong: Flying Stars Feng Shui

Xuan Kong Flying Stars Feng Shui is an essential introductory book to the subject of Xuan Kong Fei Xing, a well-known and popular system of Feng Shui, written by International Feng Shui Master Trainer Joey Yap.

In his down-to-earth, entertaining and easy to read style, Joey Yap takes you through the essential basics of Classical Feng Shui, and the key concepts of Xuan Kong Fei Xing (Flying Stars). Learn how to fly the stars, plot a Flying Star chart for your home or office and interpret the stars and star combinations. Find out how to utilise the favourable areas of your home or office for maximum benefit and learn 'tricks of the trade' and 'trade secrets' used by Feng Shui practitioners to enhance and maximise Qi in your home or office.

An essential integral introduction to the subject of Classical Feng Shui and the Flying Stars System of Feng Shui!

---

## Xuan Kong Flying Stars: Structures and Combinations

Delve deeper into Flying Stars through a greater understanding of the 81 Combinations and the influence of the Annual and Monthly Stars on the Base, Sitting and Facing Stars in this 2nd book in the Xuan Kong Feng Shui series. Learn how Structures like the Combination of 10, Up the Mountain and Down the River, Pearl and Parent String Structures are used to interpret a Flying Star chart.

(Available in 2008)

---

### Xuan Kong Flying Stars: Advanced Techniques

Take your knowledge of Xuan Kong Flying Stars to a higher level and learn how to apply complex techniques and advanced formulas such as Castle Gate Technique, Seven Star Robbery Formation, Advancing the Dragon Formation and Replacement Star technique amongst others. Joey Yap also shows you how to use the Life Palace technique to combine Gua Numbers with Flying Star numbers and utilise the predictive facets of Flying Stars Feng Shui.

(Available in 2009)

# Continue Your Journey with Joey Yap's Books

## The Art of Date Selection: Personal Date Selection

In today's modern world, it is not good enough to just do things effectively – we need to do them efficiently, as well. From the signing of business contracts and moving into a new home, to launching a product or even tying the knot; everything has to move, and move very quickly too. There is a premium on Time, where mistakes can indeed be costly.

The notion of doing the Right Thing, at the Right Time and in the Right Place is the very backbone of Date Selection. Because by selecting a suitable date specially tailored to a specific activity or endeavor, we infuse it with the most positive energies prevalent in our environment during that particular point in time; and that could well make the difference between 'make-and-break'! With the *Art of Date Selection: Personal Date Selection*, learn simple, practical methods you can employ to select not just good dates, but personalized good dates. Whether it's a personal activity such as a marriage or professional endeavor such as launching a business, signing a contract or even acquiring assets, this book will show you how to pick the good dates and tailor them to suit the activity in question, as well as avoid the negative ones too!

## The Art of Date Selection: Feng Shui Date Selection

Date Selection is the Art of selecting the most suitable date, where the energies present on the day support the specific activities or endeavors we choose to undertake on that day. Feng Shui is the Chinese Metaphysical study of the Physiognomy of the Land – landforms and the Qi they produce, circulate and conduct. Hence, anything that exists on this Earth is invariably subject to the laws of Feng Shui. So what do we get when Date Selection and Feng Shui converge?

Feng Shui Date Selection, of course! Say you wish to renovate your home, or maybe buy or rent one. Or perhaps, you're a developer, and wish to know WHEN is the best date possible to commence construction works on your project. In any case – and all cases – you certainly wish to ensure that your endeavors are well supported by the positive energies present on a good day, won't you? And this is where Date Selection supplements the practice of Feng Shui. At the end of the day, it's all about making the most of what's good, and minimizing what's bad.

(Available in 2008)

# Elevate Your Feng Shui Skills With Joey Yap's Home Study Course And Educational DVDs

## Xuan Kong Vol.1
### An Advanced Feng Shui Home Study Course

Learn the Xuan Kong Flying Star Feng Shui system in just 20 lessons! Joey Yap's specialised notes and course work have been written to enable distance learning without compromising on the breadth or quality of the syllabus. Learn at your own pace with the same material students in a live class would use. The most comprehensive distance learning course on Xuan Kong Flying Star Feng Shui in the market. Xuan Kong Flying Star Vol. 1 comes complete with a special binder for all your course notes.

## Feng Shui for Period 8 - (DVD)

Don't miss the Feng Shui Event of the next 20 years! Catch Joey Yap LIVE and find out just what Period 8 is all about. This DVD boxed set zips you through the fundamentals of Feng Shui and the impact of this important change in the Feng Shui calendar. Joey's entertaining, conversational style walks you through the key changes that Period 8 will bring and how to tap into Wealth Qi and Good Feng Shui for the next 20 years.

## Xuan Kong Flying Stars Beginners Workshop - (DVD)

Take a front row seat in Joey Yap's Xuan Kong Flying Stars workshop with this unique LIVE RECORDING of Joey Yap's Xuan Kong Flying Stars Feng Shui workshop, attended by over 500 people. This DVD program provides an effective and quick introduction of Xuan Kong Feng Shui essentials for those who are just starting out in their study of classical Feng Shui. Learn to plot your own Flying Star chart in just 3 hours. Learn 'trade secret' methods, remedies and cures for Flying Stars Feng Shui. This boxed set contains 3 DVDs and 1 workbook with notes and charts for reference.

## BaZi Four Pillars of Destiny Beginners Workshop - (DVD)

Ever wondered what Destiny has in store for you? Or curious to know how you can learn more about your personality and inner talents? BaZi or Four Pillars of Destiny is an ancient Chinese science that enables us to understand a person's hidden talent, inner potential, personality, health and wealth luck from just their birth data. This specially compiled DVD set of Joey Yap's BaZi Beginners Workshop provides a thorough and comprehensive introduction to BaZi. Learn how to read your own chart and understand your own luck cycle. This boxed set contains 3 DVDs and 1 workbook with notes and reference charts.

# Interested in learning MORE about Feng Shui? Advance Your Feng Shui Knowledge with the Mastery Academy Courses.

## Feng Shui Mastery Series™
### LIVE COURSES (MODULES ONE TO FOUR)

**Feng Shui Mastery – Module One**

## Beginners Course

Designed for students seeking an entry-level intensive program into the study of Feng Shui , Module One is an intensive foundation course that aims not only to provide you with an introduction to Feng Shui theories and formulas and equip you with the skills and judgments to begin practicing and conduct simple Feng Shui audits upon successful completion of the course. Learn all about Forms, Eight Mansions Feng Shui and Flying Star Feng Shui in just one day with a unique, structured learning program that makes learning Feng Shui quick and easy!

**Feng Shui Mastery – Module Two**

## Practitioners Course

Building on the knowledge and foundation in classical Feng Shui theory garnered in M1, M2 provides a more advanced and in-depth understanding of Eight Mansions, Xuan Kong Flying Star and San He and introduces students to theories that are found only in the classical Chinese Feng Shui texts. This 3-Day Intensive course hones analytical and judgment skills, refines Luo Pan (Chinese Feng Shui compass) skills and reveals 'trade secret' remedies. Module Two covers advanced Forms Analysis, San He's Five Ghost Carry Treasure formula, Advanced Eight Mansions and Xuan Kong Flying Stars and equips you with the skills needed to undertake audits and consultations for residences and offices.

**Feng Shui Mastery – Module Three**
### Advanced Practitioners Course

Module Three is designed for Professional Feng Shui Practitioners. Learn advanced topics in Feng Shui and take your skills to a cutting edge level. Be equipped with the knowledge, techniques and confidence to conduct large scale audits (like estate and resort planning). Learn how to apply different systems appropriately to remedy situations or cases deemed inauspicious by one system and reconcile conflicts in different systems of Feng Shui. Gain advanced knowledge of San He (Three Harmony) systems and San Yuan (Three Cycles) systems, advanced Luan Tou (Forms Feng Shui) and specialist Water Formulas.

**Feng Shui Mastery – Module Four**

## Master Course

The graduating course of the Feng Shui Mastery (FSM) Series, this course takes the advanced practitioner to the Master level. Power packed M4 trains students to 'walk the mountains' and identify superior landform, superior grade structures and make qualitative evaluations of landform, structures, Water and Qi and covers advanced and exclusive topics of San He, San Yuan, Xuan Kong, Ba Zhai, Luan Tou (Advanced Forms and Water Formula) Feng Shui. Master Internal, External and Luan Tou (Landform) Feng Shui methodologies to apply Feng Shui at every level and undertake consultations of every scale and magnitude, from houses and apartments to housing estates, townships, shopping malls and commercial districts.

# BaZi Mastery Series™
## LIVE COURSES (MODULES ONE TO FOUR)

**BaZi Mastery – Module One**
## Intensive Foundation Course

This Intensive One Day Foundation Course provides an introduction to the
principles and fundamentals of BaZi (Four Pillars of Destiny) and Destiny
Analysis methods such as Ten Gods, Useful God and Strength of Qi. Learn how
to plot a BaZi chart and interpret your Destiny and your potential. Master
BaZi and learn to capitalize on your strengths, minimize risks and downturns
and take charge of your Destiny.

**BaZi Mastery – Module Two**
## Practical BaZi Applications

BaZi Module Two teaches students advanced BaZi analysis techniques and
specific analysis methods for relationship luck, health evaluation, wealth
potential and career potential. Students will learn to identify BaZi chart
structures, sophisticated methods for applying the Ten Gods, and how to read
Auxiliary Stars. Students who have completed Module Two will be able to
conduct professional BaZi readings.

**BaZi Mastery – Module Three**
## Advanced Practitioners Program

Designed for the BaZi practitioner, learn how to read complex cases and unique
events in BaZi charts and perform Big and Small assessments. Discover how to
analyze personalities and evaluate talents precisely, as well as special formulas
and classical methodologies for BaZi from classics such as Di Tian Sui and
Qiong Tong Bao Jian.

**BaZi Mastery – Module Four**
## Master Course in BaZi

The graduating course of the BaZi Mastery Series, this course takes the
advanced practitioner to the Masters' level. BaZi M4 focuses on specialized
techniques of BaZi reading, unique special structures and advance methods
from ancient classical texts. This program includes techniques on date selection
and ancient methodologies from the Qiong Tong Bao Jian and Yuan Hai Zi
Ping classics.

# XUAN KONG MASTERY SERIES™
## LIVE COURSES (MODULES ONE TO THREE)
### * Advanced Courses For Master Practitioners

---

### Xuan Kong Mastery – Module One
## Advanced Foundation Program

This course is for the experienced Feng Shui professionals who wish to expand their knowledge and skills in the Xuan Kong system of Feng Shui, covering important foundation methods and techniques from the Wu Chang and Guang Dong lineages of Xuan Kong Feng Shui.

---

### Xuan Kong Mastery – Module Two A
## Advanced Xuan Kong Methodologies

Designed for Feng Shui practitioners seeking to specialise in the Xuan Kong system, this program focuses on methods of application and Joey Yap's unique Life Palace and Shifting Palace Methods, as well as methods and techniques from the Wu Chang lineage.

---

### Xuan Kong Mastery – Module Two B
## Purple White

Explore in detail and in great depth the star combinations in Xuan Kong. Learn how each different combination reacts or responds in different palaces, under different environmental circumstances and to whom in the property. Learn methods, theories and techniques extracted from ancient classics such as Xuan Kong Mi Zhi, Xuan Kong Fu, Fei Xing Fu and Zi Bai Jue.

---

### Xuan Kong Mastery – Module Three
## Advanced Xuan Kong Da Gua

This intensive course focuses solely on the Xuan Kong Da Gua system covering the theories, techniques and methods of application of this unique 64-Hexagram based system of Xuan Kong including Xuan Kong Da Gua for landform analysis.

# MIAN XIANG MASTERY SERIES™
## LIVE COURSES (MODULES ONE AND TWO)

### Mian Xiang Mastery – Module One
## Basic Face Reading

A person's face is their fortune – learn more about the ancient Chinese art of Face Reading. In just one day, be equipped with techniques and skills to read a person's face and ascertain their character, luck, wealth and relationship luck.

### Mian Xiang Mastery – Module Two
## Practical Face Reading

Mian Xiang Module Two covers face reading techniques extracted from the ancient classics Shen Xiang Quan Pian and Shen Xiang Tie Guan Dau. Gain a greater depth and understanding of Mian Xiang and learn to recognize key structures and characteristics in a person's face.

# Yi Jing Mastery Series™
## LIVE COURSES

### Traditional Yi Jing

'Yi', relates to change. Change is the only constant in life and the universe, without exception to this rule. The Yi Jing is hence popularly referred to as the Book or Classic of Change. Discoursed in the language of Yin and Yang, the Yi Jing is one of the oldest Chinese classical texts surviving today. With Traditional Yi Jing, learn how this Classic is used to divine the outcomes of virtually every facet of life; from your relationships to seeking an answer to the issues you may face in your daily life.

### Plum Blossom Numerology

Shao Yong, widely regarded as one of the greatest scholars of the Sung Dynasty, developed Mei Hua Yi Shu (Plum Blossom Numerology) as a more advanced means for divination purposes using the Yi Jing. In Plum Blossom Numerology, the results of a hexagram are interpreted by referring to the Gua meanings, where the interaction and relationship between the five elements, stems, branches and time are equally taken into consideration. This divination method, properly applied, allows us to make proper decisions whenever we find ourselves in a predicament.

# Date Selection Mastery Series™
## LIVE COURSES (MODULES ONE AND TWO)

### Date Selection Mastery Series Module 1

The Mastery Academy's Date Selection Mastery Series Module 1 is specifically structured to provide novice students with an exciting introduction to the Art of Date Selection. Learn the rudiments and tenets of this intriguing metaphysical science. What makes a good date, and what makes a bad date? What dates are suitable for which activities, and what dates simply aren't? And of course, the mother of all questions: WHY aren't all dates created equal. All in only one Module – Module 1!

### Date Selection Mastery Series Module 2

In Module 2, discover advanced Date Selection techniques that will take your knowledge of this Art to a level equivalent to that of a professional's! This is the Module where Date Selection infuses knowledge of the ancient metaphysical science of Feng Shui and BaZi (Chinese Astrology, or Four Pillars of Destiny). Feng Shui, as a means of maximizing Human Luck (i.e. our luck on Earth), is often quoted as the cure to BaZi, which allows us to decipher our Heaven (i.e. inherent) Luck. And one of the most potent ways of making the most of what life has to offer us is to understand our Destiny, know how we can use the natural energies of our environment for our environments and MOST importantly, WHEN we should use these energies and for WHAT endeavors!

You will learn specific methods on how to select suitable dates, tailored to specific activities and events. More importantly, you will also be taught how to suit dates to a person's BaZi (Chinese Astrology, or Four Pillars of Destiny), in order to maximize his or her strengths, and allow this person to surmount any challenges that lie in wait. Add in the factor of `place`, and you would have satisfied the notion of `doing the right thing, at the right time and in the right place'! A basic knowledge of BaZi and Feng Shui will come in handy in this Module, although these are not pre-requisites to successfully undergo Module 2.

## Walk the Mountains! Learn Feng Shui in a Practical and Hands-on Program.

 Feng Shui Mastery Excursion Series™ : CHINA

Learn landform (Luan Tou) Feng Shui by walking the mountains and chasing the Dragon's vein in China. This Program takes the students in a study tour to examine notable Feng Shui landmarks, mountains, hills, valleys, ancient palaces, famous mansions, houses and tombs in China. The Excursion is a 'practical' hands-on course where students are shown to perform readings using the formulas they've learnt and to recognize and read Feng Shui Landform (Luan Tou) formations.

Read about China Excursion here:
**http://www.masteryacademy.com/Education/schoolfengshui/fengshuimasteryexcursion.asp**

Mastery Academy courses are conducted around the world. Find out when will Joey Yap be in your area by visiting **www.masteryacademy.com** or call our office at +603-2284 8080.